Raising the Stakes

Raising the Stakes

Jerry Sherman Amid the Mad Men

Will Bunch

BRYAN BUNCH BOOKS

2017
BRYAN BUNCH BOOKS, Pleasant Valley, NY

Copyright © by Will Bunch

All Rights Reserved

BRYAN BUNCH BOOKS

ISBN-13: 978-1979437776

ISBN-10: 1979437777

Printed & bound in the United Stated by CreateSpace.

Introduction: Jerry Sherman and the (Minor) Christmas Miracle of Ernie Koy

Most of us go through life not realizing all the ripples we set off. I was thinking about that the other day with my computer on my lap and – as is always the case – a ballgame on the television. It occurred to me that I might not be so obsessed with my Philadelphia Phillies – and I definitely wouldn't have watched all 51, and counting, Super Bowls – had my life not crossed paths with a remarkable man named Jerry Sherman. I'll never know the answer to this for sure, but I wonder if instead of my passion for NBA hoops and even world soccer, I might be watching "Antique Roadshow" or listening to classical music if Jerry hadn't been in the right place at the right time – something, I later learned, he had quite a knack for.

Let me try to describe how this all happened in a woodsy country lane in Westchester County, New York, in the middle of the 1960s. In 1963, when I was 4 and my two younger siblings were close on the horizon, my parents – Bryan and Mary Bunch – moved to Shady Lane Farm Road, in a rambling ranch house with a big yard to run around with the (ill-fated) beagle that they bought me. With the Croton River and a large reservoir nearby, there were only a few scattered homes and – in the Baby Boom-era tradition – folks actually met their neighbors. A centerpiece of the neighborhood was a converted barn with high vaulted ceilings, standing atop a steep hill and overlooking a small but lush pond where my mother was always certain that I'd drowned any time I disappeared from her sight for more than 20 seconds. The old barn was actually somewhat famous – the composer Aaron Copland had recently lived there and penned some of his most famous works under the beams. When our family first arrived at Shady Lane Farm, the occupants were two writers, Antonio Barolini, an Italian poet, and his wife Helen, an acclaimed author in her own right. But not long after we moved to the neighborhood, the Barolinis checked out. Thus, it seemed a big deal when "the new people" moved in: A Manhattan public relations executive named Jerry Sherman, his wife Bobbi, their young child Emily and Bobbi's older daughter, Wendy – to be bolstered a short time later by the birth of a son, David, on a stormy March night.

Looking back through the years, you wouldn't have guessed that Jerry and my dad would have hit it off. Jerry was a brash and almost always opinionated product of the Bronx, while my dad was a somewhat shy and bookish Midwesterner, the first in our family of upwardly mobile hillbillies to attend college. But proximity meant something back then. Jerry Sherman and Bryan Bunch became friends, as did their wives Bobbi and Mary, and then one Sunday afternoon around the fall of 1965 came the knock on the door that changed everything.

It was Jerry. His TV in the big farmhouse was on the fritz – that kind of thing happened a lot back then – and his beloved New York Giants of Earl Morrell, Spider Lockhart and Tucker Frederickson were playing a big game that he just had to watch.

Now, you know the timeworn story about the dad who started dragging his son to baseball games when the kid was still wearing diapers? Well...that wasn't us, at least not before I turned 6. My father had fled the St. Louis Cardinal-crazed flatlands of the Midwest for a beatnik version of New York with cool jazz and bad poetry. I doubt that he'd watched more than a few scattered unintentional minutes of NFL football in his life, but on this Sunday he said "Sure" to Jerry Sherman knocking on the door. Most people eventually said "Sure" to Jerry Sherman. Maybe it was the blood-stained excitement of the glory days of pro football, or maybe it was the chance to pop open a libation in mid-afternoon, or maybe just Jerry's enthusiasm was contagious. But for one or all of those reasons, my dad was hooked on the New York Giants, thanks to Jerry. Sometimes Jerry came back to watch a game, but soon the Giants were on in our house every Sunday even when he wasn't around. And this first-grader wanted in on the action. By the next season in 1966, I was even listening to Marty Glickman call the home games – which were still blacked out on TV -- on the radio.

By then we'd moved away from Shady Lane Farm, to a bigger home in a more blandly suburban neighborhood called Chilmark, which wouldn't become famous until four decades later when that 1960s incarnation of the neighborhood became the fictional home of Don and Betty Draper on TV's "Mad Men." But the good news was that Jerry and Bobbi Sherman and their kids remained good friends – while sports became the focal point of my young brain. That Christmas, I reached under our twinkling tree and pulled out a slender gift. It was a signed picture of my absolute favorite player on the 1966 Giants, a young running back out of Texas named Ernie Koy. I looked at my parents with 7-year-old amazement. How did you get this? I asked.

"We didn't really get this," my dad told me. "Jerry Sherman got it." Jerry knew Ernie Koy. Jerry knew everybody, I found out.

A lot happened over the next 50 years. The Shermans abandoned suburbia to return to Manhattan and a trippy summer home on Fire Island, then ditched America altogether to spend a couple of years in Barcelona during the depths of Watergate. My love for the gridiron grew to the point of playing varsity football at a Westchester prep school, bonding with my dad at Giants games during their brief 1970s exile to the Yale Bowl, and becoming a sports fanatic in general. I went into journalism – Watergate's impact on me – and as I moved from western Pennsylvania to Alabama and back to New York and finally down to Philadelphia in search of a good story, I'd get an update from time to time on the Shermans. Jerry was doing very, very well, my parents told me, as a corporate public relations executive back in Manhattan. The last time that I saw him was around the turn of the millennium. The Shermans and my parents were – relatively speaking – neighbors again, everyone having retired to the central Hudson Valley. Jerry and Bobbi lived in a spacious home on a steep hillside; it was filled with antiques and various knick-knacks – including a knight's coat of armor that fascinated my own young children – and offered a majestic view of the river below. It reminded me, as I think back on it, of those incessant retirement-planning TV commercials about "life well spent."

Jerry Sherman died in 2013. Three years later, I found myself sitting in Bobbi Sherman's apartment just outside of Albany, near her daughter Emily and her family. There were reminders of Jerry everywhere – old-time snapshots with sports luminaries like Muhammad Ali and Patrick Ewing, a framed letter of congratulations from President Barack Obama, and this quote: "In the PR game, the days are tough, the nights are long, and the work is emotionally demanding. But it's all worth it, because the rewards are shallow, transparent and meaningless." I was there for Bobbi to pitch me on writing a book about Jerry's life. I didn't have to think about it very long.

It's a heck of a story. For one thing, Jerry had a front-row seat for one of the biggest business stories of the latter 20th Century – the corporate takeover wars involving his employer, Paramount Communications, and such charismatic players as Jerry's boss Marty Davis and suitors like Barry Diller and Sumner Redstone. But dig deeper and you realize that, in many ways, the story of

Raising the Stakes

Jerry Sherman is the bigger saga of 20th Century America: The yearnings for the American Dream that percolated in a place like the Bronx in the 1930s and '40s, an Eisenhower era that wasn't nearly as pristine as it looked on black-and-white televisions, and the birth of modern public relations in the go-go 1980s of New York. It was a time when a kid from Harrison Avenue in the Morris Heights section of the Bronx could beat the whiz kids out of Harvard and Yale on instinct and street smarts. Jerry Sherman was a master of public relations because he had mastered the art of understanding what people really wanted – whether it was a business reporter from the *Wall Street Journal* or a 7-year-old boy who wanted an autographed picture of Ernie Koy.

This is the remarkable story of his life and times.

Chapter 1: Straight Outta Harrison Avenue

It would be a cliché to say that there's nothing left of the Bronx where Jerry Sherman was born on July 16, 1930. The Bronx, where he grew up in a world of strivers and stickball, amid a Great Depression followed immediately by a World War. The Bronx, where he attended America's largest high school, which was overflowing with kids just like him, eager to break free from the urban working class and find their own personal slice of the American Dream.

But the home where Jerry grew up at 2116 Harrison Avenue was knocked down decades ago. I drove to Jerry's old block on an unseasonably cold afternoon in March 2017, trying to get a feeling for what it was like to grow up there. There wasn't a lot to see; in fact, there is no 2116 Harrison Avenue any more, just an empty alleyway between two sturdy, three-story blocks of apartments -- well-kept buildings of red brick and siding, topped by satellite TV dishes, in a street jammed with well-worn Toyotas and Hyundais. A place that was solidly in the middle of New York City's middle class. As I sat in my own car, shielded from the late-winter wind and staring into the void where Jerry, his sister and parents had lived eight decades ago, the occasional neighbor walked by. Almost all the residents were African-American — hardly a surprise in a borough that went from farmland to teeming with European immigrants to mostly blacks and Latinos in little more than a few decades.

And yet the more things change, the more they stay the same. Just a block and a half to the east, on bustling Jerome Avenue, the No. 4 train still rumbled overhead, still carrying folks to Jerry's iconic alma mater, Dewitt Clinton High School, a few stops north, or south toward Manhattan's Financial District, where Jerry would start working in journalism while still a teenager. On the surface, things look a lot different; most of the kosher delis are closed, as the line of cars waiting for drive-through orders at the McDonald's stretches out onto Jerome. The elevated trains rumble over a bizarre tableau – rows of one auto parts store after another, peddling cheap mufflers and car stereos, as young black and brown men wave their arms to passing suburbanites, promising a good deal. The people may look different, but the karma is not so different from when Jerry was born 87 years ago – except that the strivers and hustlers then were mostly Jews, most not far removed from Eastern Europe, and most funneled through the densely populated Lower East Side.

****

Many years later, this is how Pauline Sherman remembered it: Someone frantically running down East 6th Street from the little store on the corner – the store that had the only telephone on the block back in the 1920s.

"Paulie, Paulie!" the shout came. "You got a call!"

A boy named Joseph Sherman was on the other end of the line. It would prove to be an even more important call than anyone realized at the time.

She was Pauline Blaustein then, and her family had arrived in Manhattan from Hungary around the start of the 20th Century. Pauline and her siblings lived in the heart of the bustling, overstuffed Lower East Side on East 6th Street, not far from the hub of the Hungarian immigrant community on Houston Street that was known as Goulash Row or, simply, Little Hungary. Her dad operated a seltzer cart in the neighborhood; that may seem like an odd profession but in the early years of the last century there were hundreds of these on the Lower East Side, as enterprising merchants took advantage of an almost insatiable thirst among New York's Jews for seltzer, especially flavored varieties such as egg and chocolate.

It was hard work, and apparently was something of a comedown for the ambitious immigrants from Eastern Europe. The family of Pauline's mother had been middle-class furniture makers back in the home country. Her husband had emigrated to the United States ahead of her – Pauline's mom was already pregnant with her first-born, one of Pauline's older siblings – and she was shocked at conditions when she arrived in the New World.

"She gets off the boat in Lower Manhattan and she's in this tenement several flights up that they're sharing with a bunch of people, with one bathroom down the hall," her granddaughter Emily Sherman, who became a confidant later in life, remembers her saying. "She was kind of horrified, like, 'What have they done to me?'"

Eventually, Pauline's mom would take on work as a seamstress – a common profession for women in the era that was made notorious by the fire at the Triangle Shirt Factory, a typical sweatshop. But in many ways, Pauline took after her dad, whom she would later describe as "super loving, open-minded and philosophical." Pauline would develop a similar outlook on life – more accepting of social change than many in her generation. Bobbi Sherman also remembers her as an "open-minded free spirit." Upon learning that a family member was gay, Bobbi recalled in one instance, Pauline said, "if that's the way you are, then that's the way you should be."

They say that opposites attract. The young man who was on the phone that day, Joseph Sherman, from a Jewish family with roots in Russia, would prove to be the more stern disciplinarian of the new family. They decided to make their new life together in the Bronx.

Raising the Stakes

It's hard to imagine today, but less than 100 years ago the Bronx was more like a fast-developing suburb – offering what felt like a little bit of open space to immigrants and their offspring, yearning to breathe freer air than the cramped tenements and claustrophobic streets of neighborhoods like the Lower East Side. Lines of apartments, duplexes and small homes sprouted like rows of corn near the elevated trains of the Interborough Rapid Transit Co., or IRT, when the tracks for its northern extensions like the Jerome Avenue Line were laid in the early years of the 20th Century. At some unknown point in the 1920s, when the economy was booming and a right fielder named Babe Ruth was swatting home runs in the colossal new ballpark off the Harlem River, Joseph and Pauline Sherman followed that increasingly beaten down path for Jewish immigrants. Indeed, the census recorded that in 1930 – the year that Jerry was born – the Bronx was 49 percent Jewish. The South Bronx alone reported 364,000 Jewish residents. That would be the apex. For that brief moment, the Bronx was the largest Jewish city in the world.

Raising the Stakes

Those who look back on the era describe the Grand Concourse – the grand boulevard that passed massive apartment houses as it wound through the southern central Bronx on its way toward Yankee Stadium – as a kind of Champs-Élysées for American Judaism. The side streets were packed with ornate synagogues – many still stand today, converted to other uses such as day care centers – and kosher butchers, even live chicken markets, and packs of young kids playing stickball until the sun went down.

Everything we know about Jerry Sherman's childhood was fairly typical. He arrived about 15 months after his older sister, Renee, who would prove to be his only sibling. The family was religious during Jerry's youth, attending services and going through the usual rituals like bar mitzvahs. Like most kids growing up during the 1930s and '40s, in the golden age of Hollywood pictures like *Gone with the Wind*, *The Wizard of Oz* and *Casablanca*, young Jerry loved going to movies. (And hard as it is to believe now, the Bronx had roughly 1,000 motion picture houses back then, including some palatial theatres that lined the Grand Concourse.)

Raising the Stakes

And Jerry would later recall the epic stickball games in the neighborhood. Hopefully the pitcher threw the ball low, because Jerry was a short kid, the kind who fell in love with sports but was too small for any realistic dreams of playing the game professionally. One would have to imagine that growing up a short hop from Yankee Stadium in the final years of the nickel subway ride, and in the golden years when Lou Gehrig said his sad farewell and a kid named Joe DiMaggio arrived to patrol center field, also nurtured Jerry's life-long love of sports. Indeed, it eventually became a legend in the family that at some point in his youth he even found work – maybe once, maybe more – as the kid who got to change some of the numbers on the old-fashioned manual scoreboard in the House That Ruth Built. Like a long blast by Joltin' Joe into the short porch in right field, the truth of that particular tale is hard to find.

Jerry probably didn't go to too many Yankees games with his dad. Joseph Sherman found steady work as a cab driver, which meant that he worked odd hours and was gone much of the time. When he was home, Jerry's dad was clearly the disciplinarian of the family – a trait that was apparently passed down from father to son. Family legend has it that Joseph Sherman was particularly strict with Jerry's older sister, Renee.

Emily Sherman's sense is that Jerry "didn't spend a lot of time with his father – that he was working, and he was temperamental. And there was favoritism – he thought that boys were better. He thought that girls were a problem and that you have to get married. It was *Fiddler on the Roof*-ish."

Favoritism or not, Jerry seemed to bond with his more outgoing, opinionated and empathetic mother, Pauline. Years later, as a young newlywed married to Bobbi, and then as he steadily climbed up the public relations ladder in public relations, Jerry still found a few minutes to call Pauline and check up on her every single day. If Jerry's dad taught him to be strict, Jerry's mom preached tolerance, and family members said she inspired her son to be open minded like her.

Pauline would later tell her granddaughter and confidant Emily that she'd once been "a party girl" in her youth. Bobbi Sherman described her mother-in-law this way: "if you met her, she was a little old Jewish lady from Europe, that's what she looked and acted like. But she was so ahead of her time – so open, free-spirited." Eventually, life's misfortunes had even caused Pauline to reconsider her bedrock Jewish faith.

But the young strivers of the Bronx in the middle of the 20th Century never lost faith in one thing: the power of the American Dream. The social mobility promised by the United States, and especially by the polyglot of migrants who'd settled in New York, was in many cases why their families had fled the stilted societies of Europe, or elsewhere, in the first place. And there was one primary escape hatch from the lower middle class: The city's then-outstanding public schools.

And if schools were the pipeline to American prosperity, the Bronx's DeWitt Clinton High School was the supercharged funnel. In 1929, the year before Jerry was born, New York City's elite, boys-only high school moved from Manhattan to a large patch of green space on the parkland along the Mosholu Parkway in the northern Bronx. The new DeWitt Clinton High School was a tower of learning -- an imposing fortress sprawling across 21 acres, with ornate cupolas and large windows, surrounded by stately trees. It was designed by the famed New York school architect C.B.J. Snyder. The city spent the then-large sum of $3.5 million on its new school, but officials thought it was worth every penny. "This temple of education will well repay us even after we are gone, by training future generations to be good citizens," the city's then-mayor, James J. Walker, said.

The new campus was meant to accommodate 5,600 students – but enrollment swelled during the 1930s as both the Great Depression and the launch of child labor laws meant that teenagers who once might have gone to work sought instead to stay in school. By the end of the decade, some 12,000 students crammed into Dewitt Clinton's hallways, making it the largest high school in America. The place was a tribute to democracy and social mobility.

"DeWitt Clinton might be a castle, but it never had a moat, never had something to protect it like an entrance exam," Gerard J. Pelisson, co-author of the definitive history *The Castle on the Parkway: The Story of New York City's DeWitt Clinton High School and its Extraordinary Influence on American Life*, told the *New York Times*. "The school never kept out any kind of nonacademic student. It was always very open."

The authors noted that the Bronx was a magnet for immigrant families in the early 20th Century because of its affordable housing stock, and that DeWitt Clinton was almost like a country private school experience for kids coming from cramped streets and messy situations at home. "It was nice to have a different feeling than what they had at home," Paul Pitluk, who graduated from the school in 1949 and was there the same time as Jerry Sherman, told the *Times*. "The Clinton boys had a different environment — for many, an escape from a difficult neighborhood situation."

By the time that Jerry enrolled in the mid-1940s, just as U.S. involvement in World War II was winding down, the list of alumni who had already passed through the hallways of DeWitt Clinton was truly remarkable. They included the photographer

Richard Avedon, the screenwriter Paddy Chayefsky, the playwright Frank Gilroy, the Hollywood director Stanley Kramer, the radical attorney William Kunstler, actor Burt Lancaster, comic book icon Stan Lee, boxer Sugar Ray Robinson, and the *New York Times* top editor A.M. Rosenthal. Another DeWitt Clinton alumnus, in what can only be considered a bit of remarkable foreshadowing for Jerry, was Edward Bernays -- considered the father of modern public relations. Others became leaders of business, politics, or the arts.

And those were just the kids ahead of Jerry. Some of the other students roaming the hallways during his time at DeWitt Clinton in the mid-1940s included the legendary concert promoter Bill Graham, whose family had arrived in the Bronx after fleeing Adolf Hitler's Holocaust, producer Gilbert Cates, *New Yorker* cartoonist Sam Gross, the future congressman Charlie Rangel, and basketball's Dolph Schayes, among others.

There was almost something in the water at DeWitt Clinton that made people successful. That said, in such a crowded school of striving overachievers, how does a kid like Jerry Sherman coming up every morning on the No. 4 train from University Heights stand out? He probably didn't. Jerry didn't hit a growth spurt until his senior year, when he finally shot up to about 5-10. According to records he later filed with the U.S. Air Force, he reported that he'd played baseball, softball, and basketball in high school. It's not clear at what level he played and it wasn't something he would later brag about to his family. On the same military form, he reported that he was able to read, write, and speak French "fairly well" (but not fluently) and that his "talent for furnishing public entertainment" was in the area of script writing.

Jerry may have been short but was already good looking -- or at least what grown-ups might call adorable -- at that age. Once he confided to Bobbi about a time when a teacher asked him to deliver a note to another teacher. Like any kid would, Jerry opened the note and read it himself. It said: "Isn't he cute?"

But those days passed quickly: When Jerry turned 16, or roughly halfway through high school – his attention was dramatically diverted elsewhere. Tragedy had struck the Sherman household.

As Pauline would later relate to family members, Joseph Sherman had gone to the hospital for problems with ulcers. It seemed like a routine visit, and, in fact, Pauline was told to come by the next day and her husband would be discharged. But when she arrived at the appointed time, doctors pulled her aside and told her the shocking news: Her husband was dead.

Pauline was told that something had gone wrong overnight with a blood transfusion. Had it happened today, she might have sued. But it was a different era. With two years of high school left, Jerry suddenly needed to help support the family.

The year was 1946, and the job market was flooded with millions of veterans back from the European and Asian theaters. In the spirit of DeWitt Clinton alums like A.M. Rosenthal, Jerry looked toward the then-fast-growing field of journalism. The Jerome Avenue El that took him north to high school also travelled south, toward the skyscrapers of lower Manhattan. His classmates had time to play basketball after school or fill out their college applications. Jerry Sherman was off to work.

Chapter 2: Hot Dawg!

The year was 1950, and opera music blared from Café Rienzi, a brand-new joint on MacDougal Street, in the throbbing heart of Greenwich Village. A painter named David Grossblatt had just opened the establishment, which would, in the words of the *New York Times*, become "a center of Village intellectual life" for the 1950s. The Beatnik era. On most nights at the Café Rienzi, intense chess matches were interspersed with raging debates over the rise of Red-baiting U.S. Senator Joe McCarthy and other hot political topics. Patrons read one of New York City's half-dozen dailies, like the *Herald Tribune*, the *World*, or the *Telegraph*, on wooden sticks while they ate Italian pastries, drank café au lait, and smoked cigarettes.

But for a 17-year-old waitress named Bobbi Bocala, this night would be different. She would be meeting the new man in her life, a young soldier named Jerry Sherman.

Some 67 years later, Bobbi told me that Café Rienzi was where the future couple met. Then, two minutes later, she told me that maybe it wasn't how it happened. She instead remembered that as a young girl, she was working in the Bronx as a mother's helper, and she had a friend named Gil who was away in the Army, as call-ups increased again at the start of the Korean War. It was Gil who suggested that Bobbi meet his good friend, Jerry Sherman.

Eventually, Gil brought Jerry around to meet Bobbi. She says now that she knew when she met him that he was the one. "That minute I met him, it was instant," adding, as an aside, "Kids today never have that."

"That day, I didn't want him to leave," Bobbi recalled of the young, handsome soldier who showed up that day. "I told him that I was having a party that Saturday night – 'Can you come?' Of course I wasn't having a party that Saturday night." But she somehow improvised, and then later Jerry came calling at the iconic Greenwich Village coffee shop.

Still, there were clearly issues to be worked out. "He was a fascist, and I was a Communist," Bobbi said, laughing. She was only half kidding.

Raising the Stakes

The 1950s were a remarkably eventful time for Jerry and Bobbi, in an America that wasn't quite the way folks remember it. When you think of that first decade after World War II, if you weren't there – and most of us weren't – you probably think of it through the black-and-white gauze of a TV sitcom like "Father Knows Best" or "Ozzie and Harriet." Steak, mashed potatoes, and domestic tranquility of a suburban home that looked just like every other ranch house on the cul-de-sac. Cars with big fins, and the boredom of the popular father figure Dwight Eisenhower in the White House.

But the Eisenhower era was anything but tranquil for Jerry and Bobbi. Their lives were a testament to the reality that the myths of the 1950s in America are exactly that: Myths. Living in Greenwich Village, their 1950s were a time for radical politics, for difficult questions about race and marriage, and non-conformity. And yet against that backdrop, Jerry also launched a thriving career, taking the skills and the contacts he'd developed as a journalist for a leading financial newspaper and then planting his stake in the growing field of public relations.

Raising the Stakes

Jerry's youth had ended abruptly. He'd been just 16 when he showed up at the *Journal of Commerce* – which, along with the *Wall Street Journal*, was one of the city's leading business publications – and began working part-time while he continued to earn his high school diploma with his less-burdened peers at DeWitt Clinton High School. It's not clear what drew Jerry to journalism, but what was obvious was that – after his father Joseph's sudden death, presumably with little or no savings after his career as a taxi driver – that he'd need to start bringing in some money to help out his mom and his sister Renee. Newspaper work was a lot different in 1946 than it is today, when it's impossible to break into the business without a college degree, preferably from a name university, with a portfolio of clips from a summer internship. Young teens were in demand as copy boys – others who did that same job in roughly the same era as Jerry included the future Pulitzer Prize-winner Jimmy Breslin, the beat poet Allen Ginsburg, and novelist John Updike – to perform the quotidian tasks of moving the reporter's typed articles from one part of a newsroom to where the editors work. It's a task that sounds like ancient history to anyone raised only in the Computer Age. With that front foot now jammed in the door of the then-thriving news business, copy boys like Jerry then angled for writing assignments.

Although it's doubtful he realized it at that young age, Jerry's choice of the *Journal of Commerce* would broaden his knowledge of the business world and his list of contacts – starting him on the path that would lead to his career in public relations. In the 1940s, the *Journal of Commerce* still reflected its 19th Century roots – providing business leaders with basic information about what ships were coming into New York Harbor, or other fundamental facts and figures about agricultural or industrial production.

The *Journal of Commerce* was founded in 1827; crazy as it sounds today, the paper's main reporting tool was a schooner that sailed out and intercepted bigger cargo-carrying ships before they reached New York Harbor; the ensuing "scoops" gave the city's traders a heads-up on what goods would be available for auction at the docks the next day, and sometimes provided important news from Europe a day early. The 50-foot schooner – which was dubbed the *Journal of Commerce,* same as the newspaper – offered a major advantage over the much slower rowboats deployed by competing newspapers. The goal of faster communications was certainly shared by one of the *Journal of Commerce's* founders, Samuel F.B. Morse, who later in life became the father of the electric telegraph and, of course, Morse code. After a colorful history that included successfully pushing for the freedom of the slaves aboard the rebellious *Amistad* and a Civil War row with Abraham Lincoln, who shut the paper down for a time, the *JoC* still had roughly the same size circulation as the *Wall Street Journal* in those years immediately following World War II. It focused on the things it did best – covering transportation, the flow of goods, and the commodities markets.

The old newspaper was still doing pretty well when Jerry got off the subway at the nearby City Hall Station for his first afternoon of work at the paper's then headquarters at 63 Park Row in the narrow canyons of the financial district, a stone's throw from the New York Stock Exchange. World War II had made the United States the leader of the financial world, and so the *Journal of Commerce* – under the aggressive ownership of the Ridder brothers, who were also launching a chain of traditional newspapers that would extend from Philadelphia to San Jose and back – was in the process of launching an international edition. In that thriving atmosphere of growth, it wouldn't be long before young Jerry Sherman would pull down his first byline.

In Jerry Sherman's private papers, there is a thick black binder that collects most, if not all, of the bylined stories that Jerry wrote for the *Journal of Commerce*, at least in his first stint with the business newspaper, mostly in the first half of the 1950s. In his reporting, one can almost taste a slice of America in the middle of the 20th Century, covering everything from mundane corporate earnings reports to feature stories about the latest culinary treat. You could argue that the food industry was a narrow slice of a complex world, in an age with such blockbuster stories as Korea, McCarthyism, the launch of the Cold War, and the rise of Dwight Eisenhower. But the reality is that nothing better gave the flavor of life in this brave new world of Frigidaires and split-level suburbs than chronicling the business of food, and Jerry's youthful writing is drenched in the aroma of hot dogs and hot apple pie. And the Yankee-Doodle-Americana of the subject of Jerry's first known bylined article – posted on January 7, 1949, on the topic of macaroni.

"Macaroni output hits record peak," states the headline of Jerome Sherman's first article that began, "Production and sales of macaroni in 1948 were higher than any other year in the history of the industry, but some reduction appears probable in 1949 unless restrictions on exports are relaxed or removed." It turns out that people bought pasta in 1948 for the same reasons that young people live on macaroni and cheese today: It was cheap. Wrote Jerry: "The relatively low price for macaroni has been a stimulant for consumption, and with food a major portion of the budget, has helped housewives keep up with the rapidly rising cost of living."

His clip file stayed quiet until the start of 1950, when he was reporting again on the macaroni industry (which, contrary to

1949's predictions, had remained steady) but which showed his portfolio was rapidly expanding to cover commodities such as cocoa (in tight supply, with a weak crop in Brazil and an outbreak of swollen shoot disease in Africa) as well as trends in the fast-growing area of frozen foods, which billed themselves as "The Wonder Food." By October 1950, Jerry was writing feature stories, too, including a "Clerk's Day" at the Grand Union shopping chain in which the lowliest employees were rewarded with one-day stints as store managers and even as the company president.

In 1951, in paperwork that he filled out for the Air Force, Jerry listed his job at the newspaper as reporter, earning $75 a week. He wrote that his job was to "write market reports, interviews, feature stories for food, commodity and financial sections of editorial department of paper. Also handled special assignments and public relations. Also experienced in copy reading and page layout."

The facts of Jerry's rise from copy boy to reporter are lost to time, but Bobbi – who met Jerry not long after he'd finished high school – knew that after someone had referred him for work at the *Journal of Commerce,* he rapidly moved up the ranks. That was just his way. "Everything he did was very quickly," she recalled. Jerry was able to advance quickly enough that he never felt the need to go back and earn a four-year college degree, although Bobbi remembers that by the time that Jerry was in his 20s, City College was asking him to teach a class, presumably related to his journalism. His military file folder also includes a record from the registrar at New York University stating that he'd taken a course in "vocabulary improvement and development" in spring 1954 and received an "A" – but he apparently never saw a need to get a college diploma.

"There was the pressure, that you've got to start working" because his father had just died, Emily recalled her dad telling her. "There was an opening, and I think he never looked back, that was the sense that I had that, 'I needed to do this,' and it just grew and grew and grew and then clearly it morphed into public relations."

Indeed, Jerry's talents certainly made him a very good reporter but arguably even a better editor, when he tried that side of journalism. Emily noted with a laugh that the father who was constantly on her case to pick up her socks had "a regimented fastidiousness to much about his personality, which is so good for editing."

Finding success at such a young age had one other benefit: It clearly endowed Jerry with a lot of self-confidence, which became one of his hallmarks. "He had so much satisfaction from the success he had early on – he had so much pride that he started as a copy boy and then became a reporter," Bobbi recalled.

But in the 1940s and 1950s, young men launching a career typically faced an interruption for military service. Jerry would be no exception. According to his official records, Jerry's stint with the Air Force started in late 1950 with training at Brooklyn's Floyd Bennett Field. In May 1951, Jerry was sent away to MacDill Air Force Base near Tampa, Fla., where he was stationed with the 305th Bombardment Wing. In World War II, that unit had a storied history, with multiple heavy bombing runs over Germany commanded by the renowned then-Colonel Curtis LeMay, who later would become America's most hawkish general during the Cold War against the Soviet Union. But in 1951, despite the growing conflict in Korea, the unit did not immediately see combat -- and then Jerry was discharged that September.

Special orders from the Air Force command in Tampa suggest that Jerry's stint was cut short because of a "hardship discharge." The cause is not listed, but the likely reason is this: It was around this time that Jerry's mother Pauline became a widow for the second time in her relatively young life. About two years after Joseph Sherman's untimely death, Pauline had met and married a man named Sam Schneider – "an amazing guy," she confided to her granddaughter Emily years later – only to see her second husband suddenly drop dead of a heart attack. The experience changed Pauline for life; the once religious woman lost all faith in a higher power. Never again would Pauline keep kosher or follow the other tenets of the Jewish faith she'd been raised in.

Jerry clearly had been a good soldier during his brief service. When he went home that September, the commanding officer of his unit, the 4221st Armament and

Electronics Maintenance Squadron, Major William E. Swindal, wrote a letter of recommendation, stating that, "During this time he was given projects that were entirely foreign to anything he had ever done, yet with a very minimum of instructions, his results were excellent. He was entirely dependable, eager and hardworking with no regard for long hours on the job. I sincerely regret the unavoidable loss of this man to my organization..."

For all the record keeping and pomp and circumstance, his relatively short time in the military wasn't something that Jerry Sherman talked about much for the rest of his life. He probably didn't like being in the service. It had interrupted his career – and done something worse. In late 1951, Jerry came back to Manhattan with a major piece of unfinished business regarding the server from the Café Rienzi whom he had been dating, Bobbi Bocala.

A Greenwich Village bohemian, Bobbi had never been destined for a conformist life. She'd grown up in Manhattan, raised by her single mother, Dottie, who Bobbi recalls today as a "dynamo" – and not necessarily in the best sense of the word. Dottie was hard-charging at her best, and remembered even by her own granddaughter Emily as "mean": Emily laughed as she recalled meeting a cousin at a family gathering and learning their grandmother had the same effect on both of them: The ability to make them cry.

Bobbi was raised unconventionally. At first she used Dougherty as a last name before her mom married a man of Filipino descent and Bobbi took his last name of Bocala just like her younger half-sister – even though Bobbi was never formally adopted by him. Sometimes she would tell other kids she was Italian, just to throw them off. "I didn't know," she said. But family chaos didn't stop Bobbi from winning a full scholarship and becoming an excellent student at one of New York's most interesting academies, the Robert Louis Stevenson School on Broadway on the Upper West Side, an ultra-progressive school for girls.

According to the school's own history, the school was named for Stevenson at the time of its 1909 founding "in homage to his work which explored themes such as non-conformity, independent thinking and the duality of all things human." Indeed, the Stevenson school became somewhat notorious during the years that Bobbi attended in the late 1940s, as its leader Annette Rubenstein hired several teachers who'd been "blacklisted" elsewhere because of their leftist political affiliations; federal and state officials placed financial pressure on the school in an effort to force Rubenstein to resign, which she eventually would do in 1952.

Young Bobbi Bocala absorbed that world. ("It was the best education anybody can get," she would enthuse decades later.) She became a lover of the arts – both the growing poetry scene on MacDougal Street in and around Café Rienzi and also in the film industry, where she worked for a time as a script supervisor.

In Jerry's private papers, he retained a 1,800-word short story written by his wife under the name of "Bobbi Robins." In the piece, the central character is a waitress in a place very much like the Café Rienzi. She writes: "I was employed in a small coffee shop in Greenwich Village. This was the new rage, you know, with its exotic pastries, Italian coffees, and Turkish extravaganzas.

Weird paintings by the local talent were spread madly on the dingy walls. The atmosphere of this modern conception of Bohemia had settled to dust; dust and irregularly wired electric bulbs that would rather be kerosene lamps or even deny themselves as anonymous candles. Their light was a yellow, aged glow with none of the pride or vitality of Ben Franklin's discovery. In the shadows stood rickety, unstable tables littered with quaintly cracked crockery, which helped to support the artistically exorbitant prices. Yes, this was the Coffee House craze of the twentieth century."

Bobbi also became enthusiastic about the leftist politics of the time. Around the time that the Stevenson School's Rubenstein was accused of hiring Communist teachers, Bobbi recalls that her first political activity was handing out leaflets protesting the nation's best-known Red-baiter, Wisconsin Sen. Joe McCarthy.

Bobbi said she was active in a young progressive group. It wasn't a Trotskyite organization like the one that one of her best friends belonged to at the time, but it was a far-left outfit that had what might best be described as Communist leanings. With the furor over McCarthyism heating up at the dawn of the 1950s, Bobbi plunged deeper into radical left-wing politics while Jerry was off in Florida, training to defend America's interests at the dawn of the conflict in Korea.

Things happened fast. Bobbi met and quickly married one of her left-wing political allies, a young African-American man named Clarence Robins. And soon they had a daughter, Wendy, who was born on Oct. 4, 1951. It was an unconventional story – after all, interracial marriage was still banned in a number of U.S. states in the socially conservative 1950s – that had an even more unconventional ending.

When Jerry came home from Florida and learned the full story of what had happened with Bobbi, Clarence, and their daughter Wendy, he refused to accept that as a final outcome. Jerry said he was still in love with Bobbi, and he told her that she should divorce his new husband, and she and her infant daughter should come live with him. Incredibly, Bobbi complied.

"Jerry came to me and said, 'This is ridiculous, you're my wife,' in his mind" Bobbi recalled years later of the moment that changed everything. "So he said, 'You gotta come live with me, and he stole me from Clarence. He said, 'You can't be married to Clarence...I told him that I have Wendy now, and he said, 'It doesn't matter.'"

A short time later, Bobbi found herself on a train, alone, headed for the state of Alabama – a place where she had no connections but where the divorce laws were such that she could file for a divorce by herself, without Clarence's participation. (It's not clear whether the fact that Clarence was black and that Alabama was one of the states that banned interracial marriage had anything to do with this.)

When she returned, she was free to start a new life with Jerry and Wendy in the East Village. The couple made a surprising decision – again, against the backdrop of the decade associated with the social conformity of TV dinners and cookie-cutter suburban subdivisions. The couple decided not to get married, at least not right away. "We didn't believe in it," recalled Bobbi, sounding more like a 1960s flower child than a product of the staid 1940s. But it was still such an unusual decision for that time – even in New York's East Village -- that most of their friends and co-workers simply assumed that they were married, and Jerry and Bobbi didn't try to convince them otherwise. "We didn't want to shock the neighborhood again," she recalled. They wouldn't tie the knot for nearly a decade – the year before their daughter Emily was born – and when they did, it was before a justice of the peace with only a couple of close friends as witnesses.

It was difficult enough raising a biracial child in the 1950s. Bobbi said that Jerry took very quickly to his new role as a supportive stepfather. "One thing that he was not was a racist," Bobbi recalled. Frequently, it would be Jerry who would go to Wendy's schools for parent-teacher conferences or other events. Unfortunately, others didn't always share Jerry's inclusive outlook – even in progressive New York City. Bobbi recalled at least one occasion when the family was turned down for a sub-lease, because the leaseholder didn't want to rent to a couple with a biracial daughter. Occasionally, Bobbi recalled, there would be an insensitive remark about her darker skinned daughter, which she'd try to deflect with a flip retort like, "I'm the cream in the Oreo cookie."

When Jerry returned to New York City from his Air Force deployment in Florida, he picked things up at the *Journal of Commerce* as if nothing had happened. Once again, Jerry was reporting on the booming frozen food industry, including the market for frozen concentrate in orange juice, and the all- important commodity of cocoa. Meanwhile, events in the wider world often intervened in the food business that Jerry covered, whether it was the war in Korea, which caused a surge in demand for canned food for the troops, or the growing number of labor disputes at a time when union power was at its apex.

"Increasing contributions to the total volume of the nation's supermarkets are being made by frozen foods," wrote Jerry on May 8, 1952, in a piece that seems to sum up the karma of the go-go 1950s. He noted that it was increasing ad dollars on radio, in newspapers, and the fairly newfangled television that were persuading the nation's shoppers to purchase the new array of frozen foods. "Point-of-sale campaigns have brought frozen food products to the fore and have made Mrs. Housewife more frozen foods-minded." In July 1952, Jerry was reporting on the amazing progress that Birds Eye's food scientists had made in developing a frozen juice concentrate that doesn't separate in the refrigerator. Occasionally, Jerry took a break to write about the surging sales of home freezers, which made the frozen food boom possible.

"The American housewife will soon be thawing out frozen deviled crab balls, chicken turnovers and shrimpburgers," Jerry marveled in a piece that published on Oct. 9, 1952. In the piece, there are mentions of foods that today are lost to the imagination – such as "frozen imported whale steaks" as well as a shout-out to "pre-cooked breaded fish sticks," which this Baby Boomer can attest would soon become a staple of many families' diets. There is also news in the article that Birds Eye is about to unveil the pre-cooked, quick-frozen chicken pie, which, he wrote, "presents to the American housewife a product which is 'convenient, tasty, easy-to-use and easy on the pocketbook.'"

If it sounds like Jerry specialized mainly in new-age food for the "flying saucer" era, he also covered the classics, especially in this undated article that appears to be from the mid-1950s about the skyrocketing popularity of the hot dog, something that we might take for granted today. "Hot Dawg!", his article begins – a sign that Jerry enjoyed taking a diversion from some of the dryer reports about rising cocoa prices. (The story's sub-headline hails "Davey Crockett – with mustard" – a nod to the way that television had helped to market the frankfurter to America's kids in the '50s.) His lengthy report notes that, "Frankfurter-feastin' Americans ate enough hot dogs during the peak sales season to construct a chain of the wieners wrapped around the world at the Equator 10 times." Crunching the numbers, Jerry estimated that the total hot dog consumption for 1955 would hit 8,145,000,000 wieners. And he traces the treat's origin to 16th Century Frankfurt, then across the pond to its American breakout at the 1904 World Exposition in St. Louis, through the baseball parks of his own youth, where the treat caught on at the Giants' Polo Ground in upper Manhattan, and right up to 1955's

"Hot Dog Davey," the promotional tie-in to the TV frontiersman.

Individually, Jerry's articles from the mid-1950s – about a new ad campaign for the California walnut industry, or reports from the American Meat Institute that the use of lard was making a comeback – might seem like disposable pieces of forgettable information on dead tree bark, memorializing a long-lost time. But read in their entirety, Jerry's *Journal of Commerce* clip file tells a fairly compelling story of a world in the midst of a rapid transition. It's easy to forget now, but the rise of the supermarkets with their big parking lots and gleaming aisles stocked with a once unimaginable array of products replacing the familiar but suddenly quaint corner grocery or country store meant dramatic changes not just in the ways that Americans shopped but in how they lived. For what was increasingly becoming a more centralized industry of food manufacturers such as General Mills or Kraft or Campbell's Soup, the race was on to freeze or at least mass-produce everything from "frozen bread" (an obsession, as Jerry reported, of Admiral Richard Byrd of South Poleconquering fame) to whale steaks and shrimpburgers. For the small grocers and local bakers who'd been the pillars of their local communities in the early 20th Century, the fight was one for survival.

In one shockingly prescient article from July 13, 1953, Jerry talks to food industry experts who argue that supermarkets will need to be increasingly mechanized to record a profit and who predict a futuristic world in which "(t)he packages move in front of an electronic device which 'reads' the price on each package, adds up the total and makes available a printed receipt." That was written nearly four decades before barcode scanning became a regular way of supermarket shopping in America. Sadly, the article's concluding prediction, that a conveyer belt would then whisk the customer's purchases out to the parking lot, has not come to pass.

In October 1953, Jerry covered the annual dinner of the National Sugar Brokers Association at Manhattan's Biltmore Hotel, where the industry's newish concern was one that will seem familiar to today's readers: Doctors and other experts were beginning to warn consumers that too much sugar consumption was making them overweight. "The public is led to believe one of the best ways to become and stay thin is to eat less sugar," an alarmed H. Beach Carpenter, president of the American Sugar Refining Co., told the gathering. He said the industry would counter that viewpoint with a campaign that "will also endeavor to point out new uses for sugar."

In the mid-1950s, Jerry covered the "breaded-shrimp" boom (a product that had barely existed five years earlier), the debut of a large, glamorous Acme supermarket (a "super-duper 'Super'") in Ohio that even had "a sizable Kiddie Korral and an electric horse to interest youngsters." One of the biggest trends that Jerry covered for the *Journal of Commerce* in the mid-1950s was America's sudden love affair with pets, as families became more affluent and homes became more spacious; one 1953 article notes that production of cans of dog and cat food had doubled in just the previous five years, with American families adding some 900,000 new dogs every year during the mid-'50s.

The explosion of television was also clearly on the minds of both food merchants and retailers. In January 1954, as Jerry reported, NBC-TV announced it was working with some 20,000 food merchants across America on a promotional tie-in called the "Star Value Parade," which would link its advertisers to stars such as Bob Hope, Jimmy Durante, Wally Cox, Roy Rogers, Kate Smith, Sid Caesar, and Imogene Coco. And when Americans weren't on their living room sofa watching "I Love Lucy," "Your Show of Shows," or Uncle Miltie, they were increasingly hitting the road on the new turnpikes, even before Eisenhower launched the interstate highway system.

One article from June 1955 described how industry officials were looking at new ways to cash in on picnic and barbecue items to address that growing craze. That same month, Jerry reported on the surge in roadside ice cream shops, many of which sold the newfangled soft-serve ice cream that had emerged from Army mess halls during the war years. "Ice cream-eating Americans will spend more than $1.5 billion for their frozen delicacy delights this year," he wrote, "but an increasing percentage of this figure will be accounted for by the soft-serve variety."

Ironically, later that same month he was covering candy makers who – like their cousins in the sugar trade – were increasingly alarmed by what they came to see as "calorie phobia," or Americans' increasing obsession with remaining thin. "H.L. Mencken once commented that the really enjoyable things in life are either immoral, illegal, or fattening. This bit of philosophy is challenged by the National Confectioners' Association which says 'taint so! Candy is not only 'really enjoyable,'" vows the organization, but also is good for you." Jerry wrote that industry officials hoped to promote the "energy-building" qualities of candy.

By 1955, the 24-year-old Jerry was increasingly hitting the front page of the *Journal of Commerce*. That was the case on February 19, 1955, when he appeared above the fold with a piece headlined, "U.S. Firms Push Planting of Cocoa in Latin America," which noted that "United States cocoa and chocolate manufacturers, plagued by high cocoa bean prices, are expected to turn more toward Central and South American producing areas for a bigger share of their requirements." The article was surrounded by a slew of stories about trade and tariffs at the moment that the United States, in the relative peace and stability of Eisenhower's America, was becoming the world's largest economy.

Meanwhile, Jerry was building something of his own during those youthful years at the *Journal of Commerce*: His Rolodex (which, for anyone under the age of 40, was that flippy thing of index cards with dozens of phone numbers). Every assignment brought him closer to the industry officials who would ultimately help him in the next phase of his career. But he also forged a close network of connections with the flood of young journalists who swamped New York City, the booming media capital of the free world. Some of those ties were forged at the rubber chicken banquets or industry trade conferences that he covered, but some of his closest friendships – ones that would prove valuable to him for the rest of the 20th Century – were created by his long affiliation with the New York Financial Writers Association.

The association was still a fairly young organization at the time that Jerry joined it. It had been founded in 1938 by a bevy of financial journalists from the most prestigious outfits including the *Wall Street Journal*, the *New York Times*, the *New York Herald Tribune* and the Associated Press, among others. The rationale for the group was a simple one; in 1938, as the aftershocks of the Great Depression continued to rattle most everyday American households, average citizens continued to hold Wall Street in low regard, and financial journalists – many of whom had not seen the great crash of 1929 coming – were not thought of much better. Indeed, the idea of an association to help rebuild confidence in financial journalism had support from many titans of the New York Financial District, but that support didn't translate into many dollars at first. That's why the idea of holding an annual follies type of show – similar to what the Gridiron Club was doing with political journalists in Washington, D.C. – electrified the New York financial crowd. The first show at the Hotel Astor – which charged attendees $10 a pop, which was a lot of money in the late 1930s – included musical numbers that satirized the likes of Neville Chamberlain, Franklin Roosevelt, Josef Stalin, Benito Mussolini, and Adolf Hitler, among others. Even then, there were no sacred cows.

Jerry would have still been a teenager – a cub reporter getting his very first bylines – when he started participating in the group's annual December follies, in the late 1940s. By then the Financial Writers Association had relaxed its rule to include journalists on the growing business beat, and eventually it would even allow people like Jerry who would leave the profession to stay involved as associate members. But by the time Jerry moved on from the newspaper world for his next career phase, he'd already left an indelible mark on the association – a mark that friends would still talk about decades later. This may not have been the most important moment of Jerry's life story, but it was arguably the most hilarious: His eight-year stint as one of the writers group's Follies Girls.

A glowing article in the program for the 50th Anniversary Dinner hailed Jerry as one of the best to ever don a wig and pull on a dress to sing and dance in full drag in a time when only a handful of actual women worked in the financial press. The article by Roberta C. Yafie lists Jerry along with his partners in crime – Peter Earle, Art Samansky, and George Auerbach – as "among the sexiest and most outrageous stars to hit the stages of the hotels Astor, Commodore, and Sheraton Centre."

Jerry told Yafie that "it's the only time in my life that I shaved twice a day." In hindsight, it's hardly a shock that Jerry – with those good looks that had caused his high school teachers to pass notes about him, especially in his early 20s with his curly hair, sharp features, and eagerness to please the more established names in the trade – would be singled out for the drag performance. Years later, he and the other Follies Girls clearly got a kick out of relating the adventures of their brief double life – learning how to race to the restroom in their high heels, dolling up in a boa and long white gloves, or (in the wake of the Fanne Foxe scandal that shook Washington in the early 1970s) learning the art of the striptease. "Those were the days when men were men and men were women, when the worse the singing voice, the better the chance of a solo," Yafie wrote in 1988. "But good legs still counted even then."

Jerry's designated role as Miss America, which he reportedly did for eight years, was considered a show-stopper. It all culminated in his final performance in 1956, which became the stuff of legend. "He received flowers from an unknown admirer," Yafie wrote. "And more."

"I came backstage to get undressed, and I was in my Miss America costume, when a financial editor from one of the most prominent publications in the city was attracted to me in a very serious manner, and decided that he wanted to realize his fantasies and chased me around the dressing room for about 10 minutes," Jerry related more than three decades later. "He was smashed, without a doubt. That smashed I wasn't."

For longtime friend Myron "Mike" Candell, a veteran financial journalist who would later help start business coverage for CNN when it launched in the 1980s, the episode is the quintessential story about Jerry. "Jerry was a very good-looking guy," recalled Candell, who also did a stint as one of the Follies Girls, and so in drag "he made a perfectly attractive woman." But the episode of the sloshed business editor hitting on him "was so traumatic for him."

Still, to hear Jerry talk about it, he seemed to relish the attention that came with his role, recalling how he was feted after the show at a party that was sponsored by a big oil company. "I mean, you talk about star power,' he recalled. "I didn't even have a speaking role, right? I was just Miss America of 1956. I walked out into that place after the show, out of costume, and women were telling me how gorgeous I was."

Only one person, it seems, was not a particular big fan of Jerry's role as Miss America: Bobbi Sherman. Jerry's partner had watched the 1956 performance, and she was horrified. "She said, 'Never do I want to see you dressed as a woman again,'" Jerry recalled. It was hardly the end of his relationship with the New York Financial Writers Association; at that 1988 dinner, Jerry would become one of just 15 people honored with a Distinguished Service Award, honoring his commitment to the group that was four decades old at the time. Still, Jerry's last night in a dress also marked a much more important time of transition. Jerry – despite his large clip file back at the *Journal of Commerce* on Park Row – was only 26 now, and he was in the process of making the change that would ultimately define his long career.

Jerry's initial stint with the *Journal of Commerce* ended around 1955. It was around that same time that he showed up as a kind of U.S.-based columnist for the London-based trade publication *Confectionary Manufacturing*, which covered the global candy industry. Specifically, he covered "The Confectionary Industry Abroad," posting reports on "rocketing" candy sales at American chain stores or the impact of U.S. tariff policy. In September 1955, he reported in the column that, "Meat fats, those rendered from the fatty tissues of meat animals as a by-product of meat packing, are finding increasing usage in candies and other confections in this country. This increased popularity is due directly to the application of technical advances in their processing to overcome certain inherent shortcomings and to fit them to the specialized uses of the confectioner." That July he wrote on an increasingly familiar topic: How "the spread of diet fads" had led the industry to focus on new tactics to boost "impulse sales" at supermarket cash registers.

The reports for Britain's candy makers weren't Jerry's only foreign entanglements during the 1950s. As a leading American journalist covering the ups and downs of the cocoa trade, Jerry's reporting seemed to attract intense interest from officials in the West African British colony that would soon become an independent Ghana. In February 1955, the unnamed "Permanent Secretary" for the Ministry of Trade and Labour in the capital city of Accra wrote to Jerry, in perfect British bureaucrat-ese, that "I am to say it is regretted that it is not practicable owing to the numerous other heavy commitments for this Ministry to prepare for your information a detailed report on the entire cocoa marketing arrangements in the Gold Coast and a statement on possible future plans." Two years earlier, the lead story in Accra's English-language newspaper *The Spectator*, under the banner headline "Tight Cocoa Supplies Expected," lifted Jerry's Manhattan-based reporting and admitted as much in a note that "The following article is lifted wholly from the *Journal of Commerce* dated April 20 1953 and published in New York. Incidentally it was contributed by an expert at a time Government was reducing the farmer's price here" – implying that the African cocoa growers should have been paid more. The piece is bylined "Jorome Sherman."

Interestingly, the idea to make the leap into PR may have sprung from Jerry's own reporting for the *Journal of Commerce* – as he watched the then-newish notion of using specialists in what would someday be called "spin" take hold among business executives who were flush with cash in the post-war economic boom and were looking for new ways to win over customers and continue to expand their markets.

On Jan. 26, 1954, Jerry published an item in his food-merchandising column that noted the National Association of Food Chains was about to hold a clinic to teach its members how to make better use of this new approach to influencing public opinion. The event, Jerry wrote, quoting the association president, "demonstrates the extent to which the industry has come to regard 'good public relations as good business.'" The panels aimed to show the food executives how forging good relationships with the growing worlds of newspapers and radio could help them in the marketplace.

Despite his growing clip file, Jerry was still a young man – just 24 years old at the time of that article – and clearly pondering the wide-open potential of a new field, especially now that he was supporting a family. "He made that transition to make money," Bobbi recalled.

Today, much of what we know – or what we think we know – about the public relations industry in New York in the 1950s and 1960s dovetails with television's "Mad Men," which focuses on the related world of advertising during that period amid a smoky haze of clever marketing campaigns, with a boozy and too often bawdy backdrop. The gin-soaked atmosphere in Midtown Manhattan portrayed on AMC's long-running TV series was real; but – more so than advertising – public relations in the 1950s was a wide- open and practically new field, full of fresh opportunities for a young and ambitious practitioner such as Jerry Sherman to plant his flag.

Remember Edward L. Bernays, the so-called "father of public relations" who – just like Jerry – had earned his diploma from DeWitt Clinton High School in the early years of the 20th Century? Bernays – a native of Austria and a relative of famed psychologist Sigmund Freud, who had developed his own ideas about how psychology could alter public opinion – was still practicing in the latter stages of his career in Manhattan when Jerry was starting out. It had been in 1923 that Bernays had published his groundbreaking book, *Crystallizing Public Opinion*, which argued that public relations professionals were needed as a kind of middleman who could not only put corporations or politicians in the best possible light but also help interpret for business and political leaders what the public wanted. Bernays called this the two-way street of communication.

Ironically, one of Bernays' goals seemed to be putting a positive spin on the art and science of public relations itself, which was not an inconsequential question in the middle years of the 20th Century.

With the creation of global mass media – large circulation urban newspapers, followed by radio in the 1920s and '30s, with television looming on the horizon – there was also increasing concern about the rise of propaganda, starting with World War I and expanding with the advent of Fascism, Soviet Communism, and other totalitarian political movements. During World War II, the United States and its allies sought to be savvier about using modern persuasion tactics to rally the public to support the fight against Fascism. In Washington in 1942, the Franklin Roosevelt administration launched the Office of War Information as a vehicle to tell the public that the war effort was going well – and to occasionally censor news reports that suggested the opposite. The end of the global conflict three years later freed up veterans of America's war information machinery to become salesman for the virtues of capitalism at a moment when the economy was booming.

And the American business community was more than eager to have someone tell its story. As the Great Depression ravaged the nation in the 1930s, the reputation of U.S. capitalism had suffered greatly – so it's not surprising that the captains of industry began looking to people like Bernays and other practitioners of the new science of spin to try to turn things around. As related in a history of American PR by the Museum of Public Relations, the National Association of Manufacturers, or NAM, became the first industry trade association to create a PR department during the depths of the Depression, launching a 13-year-long effort to make the battered American public feel better about Big Business. Its PR crusade "included movie shorts, leaflets, a radio serial ('The American Family Robinson') and a daily column."

But the early 1950s were the moment when PR came of age in America. That period saw the creation of two of the nation's large and iconic public relations companies – Edelman in 1952, followed by Burson-Marsteller in 1953 – and would later see PR become a multi-national business with the birth of Hill & Knowlton. Equally important, the men – and they were still mostly men – who practiced public relations increasingly saw their work less as a dark art and more as a profession, with its own ethics and standards. The Public Relations

Society of America, or PRSA, had launched in 1947 as the industry's first trade association, while the International Association of Public Relations began in 1955; in addition, there was a growing cottage industry of PR industry conferences and books about best practices. In short, PR was seen as an exciting new industry at an exciting time for America, just victorious in a global war and now the world's most prosperous nation. It was the perfect place for a young Jerry Sherman – always a salesman at heart, as the former Bobbi Bocala could certainly attest – to make his mark on the world.

Unfortunately, neither his personal papers nor his family members' recollection shed a lot of light on when Jerry took the plunge into PR, or some of the work that he did for several PR shops before he decided to hang up his own shingle with his firm, Jerry Sherman Associates. Even so, he remained active in the field of publishing as a major investor in the 1960 launch of the *Vending News*, the trade newsletter for what was a booming industry at the dawn of that new decade. A prospectus for the new publication in Jerry's files suggests big ambitions both for the new journal and the rapidly expanding industry that it covered.

"The challenge of the 1960's and a market highlighted by dynamic sales expansion creates a combination every marketing symposium talks of as the ideal situation," the prospectus states. "That's the true description for the automatic vending industry, destined to grow into one of the most effective and profitable distribution and sales channels for consumer goods. Automatic vending is the retailing of products through the use of coin-operated machines. And only the limits of Man's ingenuity and knowledge can contain the growth and sophistication of the machine that replaces him. In the vending trade, expansion is the password of today. Even greater growth will be the theme of tomorrow. Since World War II, automatic retailing has already grown out of the novelty class to take its place in the forefront of the service trades in the food and beverage fields." The ambitious goal was to publish separate editions for key regions on the East Coast.

Vending machines were arguably in their heyday in the late 1950s and early 1960s.

Raising the Stakes

After a fairly wild period of experimentation, highlighted most famously by the Automat restaurants in New York City, Philadelphia, or elsewhere, where patrons were dispensed a sandwich or hot soup from a slot, the industry was focused in the mid-20th Century on the core products such as bottled soda pop, candy bars, and, of course, cigarettes.

The first issue of the *Vending News* appeared on March 14, 1960. In a front-page editorial, the paper told its audience in the vending world that "(y)ou will be hearing a lot more about us. You will come in contact with a lot of our people. We know that at first you will read the newspaper as a curiosity. But this is just the way we want it." As promised, the New York edition offered news on just about anything that might be of even passing interest to a vending machine executive, including the fact that New York city government was accepting bids on vending contractors for key municipal buildings and the clearly disappointing revelation that the sprawling new—and, as it turned out, short-lived-- Freedomland amusement park in the Bronx would not have vending machines. The paper contained an upbeat report for vending in the New York City subways, where ridership was on the increase again and prices from soda machines had doubled from a nickel to a dime.

Even in this fairly mundane trade newspaper, the optimism of the early 1960s is something palpable. And Jerry Sherman would come to embody that spirit – during one of the more remarkable decades in American history, and beyond.

Chapter 3: Fanfare for the Common Man

The 1960s were a heady time, for an America about to elect the youthful and charismatic John F. Kennedy to the White House, and also for Jerry Sherman. It didn't hurt that his beloved sports teams were experiencing their glory days in the Bronx, both the Giants with its stars Y.A. Tittle, Frank Gifford, and Sam Huff winning the 1959 NFL championship and the Yankees in the midst of a remarkable stretch in which they reached the World Series 14 out of 16 seasons. But mainly it was because he was establishing his niche as a PR man and ready to expand his family. At the start of the 1960s, Jerry joined the rush of city dwellers seeking wide open spaces in the rapidly expanding suburbs, moving with Bobbi and Wendy to New City, New York, an upscale suburb in the heart of Rockland County, about 25 miles north of midtown Manhattan and across the Hudson River. Along with the move, this was the time when Bobbi and Jerri finally tied the knot and made things official, and also marked the looming arrival of their daughter Emily, who would be born August 6, 1961.

Other than his brief stint with the Air Force in Tampa, it was the first time that Jerry had lived outside of the congested streets of Bronx and Manhattan, and by all accounts he adjusted to his new life as a suburban professional. In typical fashion, he became the leader of the nightly poker game on the rush-hour New Jersey Transit train.

Jerry plied his trade as an associate for several large PR concerns in and around New York's Madison Avenue for roughly a decade. Other than a large file concerning his work for the *Vending News*, he saved few records of those years in which he laid the foundation of his long career in public relations, and the specifics of his resume from that time are forgotten even by his close family members. In early 1962, he was working for a mid-sized public relations outfit called Farley Manning Associates – a fact that's confirmed by a membership roster for the World Trade Club of New York, an affiliate of the Commerce and Industry Association of New York, which listed Jerry as a member. The agency's founder Farley Manning, was – like many of the "Mad Men" of the early 1960s – a tall, craggy-faced veteran of World War II who'd served as a major under the legendary Air Force general James Doolittle, best known for the daring 1942 bombing raid on Tokyo and other major Japanese cities that was considered an early turning point in the American war effort. Located at 342 Madison Avenue, Farley Manning Associates was a logical stepping-stone for Jerry; many of its clients were in the food industry, and the office included a large test kitchen.

It was around the time that he was working for Farley Manning that Jerry, Bobbi, and Emily Sherman moved back across the Hudson to the Crotonville section of Ossining – which is when they become neighbors of the author's parents and their own growing brood, a long stone's throw down the street on Shady Lane Farm Road.

Why did the Shermans move? Bobbi and other family members aren't exactly sure: Westchester – with its New York Central express commuter trains into midtown Manhattan – may have just been an easier commute, but it also may have been the opportunity to live in a truly spectacular home in a unique neighborhood. Many years afterward the prior occupant of the house

– award-winning author Helen Barolini – wrote an article for the *New York Times* relating her joy at seeing it for the first time in 1960 and learning that it belonged to Aaron Copland, the renowned composer of such works as "Fanfare for the Common Man" and "Appalachian Spring" (who also fit with Bobbi's political leanings, since he was accused of Communist ties during the McCarthy years.)

"His home was a remodeled barn - a dignified white structure on a rise above the main house, Waterloo Place, of the old Herbert property," Barolini wrote in 1985. "We walked into the magnificent space of the great room with its huge supporting beams and hand-pegged flooring and were faced by a very high enclosure around a window seat that looked out on a hill of daffodils. Breaking the two-story open space at one end of the room was the balcony that led to the sleeping quarters. In the middle of the room was a fieldstone fireplace. In the far corner was the composer's grand piano. It was, and remains, a picture of beauty and serenity that never leaves me."

Barolini also recalled that the novelist John Cheever lived in the adjoining neighborhood and that occasionally Cheever – whose writing would become indelibly linked with 1960s suburbia – would wander over a large meadow and frequently stop and have a drink with Helen and her husband, the Italian poet and novelist Antonio Barolini. She said that on one of his visits, Cheever even shared an idea he had for a short story about a suburbanite who decided to cross the county by swimming in all of its pools, which of course would in a couple of years be published as "The Swimmer," arguably one of the America's greatest-ever short stories.

Barolini said she could understand why the place had inspired an artist like Copland. "The secluded road to Shady Lane Farm," she wrote, "lined with wild iris in spring, tiger lilies in summer, and thickets of vines and wild berry bushes, led to rock outcroppings and settings of such natural beauty and quiet that it is inevitable to think of the Brooklyn-born Copland responding to it."

My family had moved to a rambling ranch house on a sloping hillside off Shady Lane Farm Road a couple of years before the Shermans arrived. My parents recall the rustic charm of a neighborhood of old stone fences that clung to its rural qualities even as suburbia was beginning to sprout all around it. Perhaps for that reason, and with its diverse and unplanned housing stock, Shady Lane Farm had a true eclectic nature. While the artistic Copland and the Barolinis along with the nearby Cheever (who, my dad recalls, used to meet up with Tony Barolini in the woods, somehow with alcohol involved) put the neighborhood on the cultural map, other residents my folks met in those years included an ex-prize fighter, a "pair of crazy psychiatrists," and the dad of a pre-school playmate of mine who was described as "a conductor"; my parents pictured him waving a baton like Copland but in fact he punched tickets on the old New York Central railroad. (Indeed, at the foot of the hill near the Hudson River sat Crotonville, a struggling low-income community.) My father was a school textbook editor for the publishing house known then as Harcourt Brace, and my mom was raising me and my newborn sister Sally.

So when the newly arrived Shermans supplanted the Barolinis in the old barn, my parents followed the neighborhood tradition and showed up on an autumn Sunday afternoon with a big plate of cookies. The timing turned out to be less than ideal. While my mom and dad introduced themselves to Bobbi and met her daughters Wendy and Emily, they heard the sound of a TV set downstairs. The Giants were playing that given Sunday, and Jerry was not to be interrupted. At some point – probably halftime – Jerry finally ambled up the stairs, said a quick hello, and returned to the football game. It didn't seem to be an auspicious introduction.

But it would be the very next Sunday when – as noted earlier in the introduction – Jerry's TV went on the fritz and he called up my dad to ask if he could hang out for the next three hours or so and watch his beloved Bronx gridders. My father sat down with him, poured a libation or two, and realized, he recalled years later, that "I was hooked" on pro football. Indeed, it was several more weeks before Jerry's television was fixed, and the NFL tradition was locked in. At some point, even this then-6-year-old started paying attention to coach Allie Sherman (no relation) and his woeful squad.

Soon, Jerry was inviting my dad to take part in a regular poker game that he hosted at the old barn ("I lost money, of course," he said) and the Shermans and the Bunches became fast friends; an old college chum of my dad, Steve Von Molnar, a top physicist for IBM, had also recently moved to northern Westchester with his wife Jean and their young children, and, once introduced, the Von Molnars and Shermans also hit it off instantly, despite the fact that that Steve – brilliant, still bearing the accent of his native Germany – could be just as stubborn and opinionated as Jerry. My parents recalled that this was just Bobbi and Jerry's way, that they simply made friends with the people they met, regardless of their background or station in life – restaurant owners and restaurant waiters, animal trainers, the cabin boy on a cruise.

Football and poker weren't the only things that the Shermans taught my parents, who'd both grown up in Peoria, Illinois, and didn't get their first bite of the Big Apple until after their marriage in 1958. They still remember the Sunday that Bobbi and Jerry invited them over for their first exposure to bagels and lox. They were obviously a hit – my dad was on his third bagel when Jerry leaned over and told him, "You're only supposed to eat one." ("I thought they were like donuts," my dad recalled decades later, still slightly embarrassed.). The moment was pure Jerry, though; he was never shy about telling people when he thought they were doing something wrong. "He treated everybody like children, and he treated his children very firmly," Mary Bunch said. "If he didn't like something that you were doing, he'd say, 'Why are you doing that?'"

One memorable story from that era, according to my dad, involves Jerry and the regular poker game that he discovered on his new commute into Manhattan, aboard the New York Central's Hudson River line. A few days later, my dad saw Jerry in the neighborhood, and he was boasting about how much money he was winning. The next time my father saw his new neighbor, Jerry was not nearly as upbeat. "They'd skinned him alive!" Bryan Bunch recalled. Jerry's lifelong love affair with poker hadn't stopped him from falling for the oldest kind of hustle around. (It was also, according to Jerry's friends, a rare instance of bad luck. My dad also recalled another – more typical – moment for Jerry at a New York charity dinner with a raffle for a week's vacation in Italy's Umbria region that Jerry won; a minute later the event announced its second raffle – an enormous basket of booze and other goodies – and Jerry won that, too.)

Of course, Jerry's exploits at bar-car poker shouldn't obscure the primary reason for the move to the suburbs: His family was expanding, and his kids were happy to grow up amid the fresh air and green lawns. For young Emily the life in the converted barn provided the kind of faded-color Kodak memories that typify the Baby Boom generation – running down the big staircase under those high ceilings to find a shiny new red bicycle under a Christmas tree.

On March 22, 1967, David Sherman was born. Ironically, a sidebar to that event – the fact that when Jerry drove Bobbi to the hospital for the delivery, they dropped off 5-year-old Emily to stay with my family – left an indelible impression on everyone involved. Emily made sure that she brought some bagels along, concerned that the Bunch family would not have anything appropriate for breakfast. Our family had moved to a new neighborhood nearby in Briarcliff Manor, and a half-century later Emily still remembers the strangeness of waking up in our unfamiliar house (and I remember it, too). Weirdly, everyone also remembers that my parents rushed out that morning to do something that otherwise they never did, which was to buy more bagels, which were a staple in the Sherman household and which they assumed would make Emily feel at home. It's strange what people remember.

In the weeks before David's arrival, Jerry also made a bold career move. By August 1966, Jerry had made at least one change, according to the *New York Times*, which reported that he had been hired by Arthur Behrstock Associates, another public relations firm run by a veteran of the U.S. wartime propaganda experts in the Japanese Theater. For unknown reasons, however, that stint was short-lived; in December 1966, the *Times* ran a second short item, this time stating that Jerry had opened his own firm, Jerry Sherman Associates. With two young children at home and a teenaged stepdaughter, Jerry was taking the big leap of going into business for himself.

As Jerry branched out on his own, he relied heavily on the network of friends and contacts that he'd built up through the *Journal of Commerce* and the New York Financial Writers Association. One was his longtime pal Myron "Mike" Candell, who'd succeeded him in the show's Follies Girls. Just like Jerry, Candell had decided for a time in the late 1960s to branch out on his own, launching his own publication called the "Wall Street Letter."

At the time, Jerry was ensconced in new offices for his PR firm at 200 West 57th Street just around the corner from Carnegie Hall. It was a three-office suite, Candell recalled, and some of the space on the floor was empty. Jerry offered to let Candell move in and use the empty space to get his newsletter – which covered the business doings of New York's throbbing financial center – off the ground. Soon, Candell had moved in a small staff, and they turned Jerry on to the massive overstuffed sandwiches that came from the iconic Gaiety Delicatessen, which was a block away on 56th Street, forerunner of the similarly meat-piling Carnegie Deli.

Over the overflowing pastrami, Candell's crew launched a weekly after-work poker game that Jerry eagerly joined; the weekly event became something of an institution for the men, a socially acceptable vice at the peak of the real-life "Mad Men" world. If Jerry had a hobby – or, yes, vice – back in those years, it was definitely gambling. Family members recalled that Jerry's father, Joseph Sherman, had been something of a gambler, and he had passed the habit down to his son. In addition to his poker games, Jerry liked to visit the track from time to time. The era of widespread casino gambling was still a couple of decades away, but when it arrived – Bobbi recalled – he loved to spend time on the gaming floors there.

Recalled Emily: "I have vivid memories – it was the very late 1960s because we had already moved back to the city – and there would be these poker games. I was probably six. I would go to sleep and then I would wake up and they would still be at the table and I was like, 'Oh my God, the sun is up!'"

Raising the Stakes

But by the second half of the 1960s, two-martini lunches and the haze of tobacco smoke was already moving to the rear in an age of bellbottoms, Nehru jackets, and heightened social consciousness. The liberal ideas that had fueled the Shermans in their youth were now erupting in increasing opposition to the Vietnam War and a new push for civil rights.

As Jerry built his public relations business, there were also opportunities for what nowadays might be called "corporate social responsibility." Of all the work that Jerry did with his own PR shop in the late 1960s, no client was the source of greater pride than the groundbreaking Daniels & Bell, which in 1971 became the first black-owned brokerage to gain a seat on the New York Stock Exchange. Indeed, the Daniels & Bell file is one of the few that Jerry preserved from that period, and Bobbi still recalled his enthusiasm for the clients decades later. It certainly was a remarkable achievement. At the time, the New York Stock Exchange had been around for 179 years, and for most of those years African-Americans were kept far from the pinnacle of American capitalism. More typical was the experience of the family of one of the firm's two main founders, Travers J. Bell, who grew up in a Chicago housing project; according to the *New York Times*, his father worked in the operations department of the Chicago office of Dempsey Tegler & Company and was able to get his son a messenger's job. But opportunities were finally opening up for enterprising young blacks with the arrival of the 1960s, and Travis Bell Jr. came back from college and quickly became a vice president of the Chicago firm. When he launched his new brokerage, Bell was only 30 and his partner, Willie L. Daniels, was just 33.

The arrival of Daniels & Bell on Wall Street was the kind of feel-good story that a PR man like Jerry Sherman loves to tell. Even though the young firm only had $175,000 in capital, the civil rights shockwaves of that era – culminating with urban riots and the assassination of Martin Luther King – had encouraged some of the bigger names in the world of finance, such as Chase Manhattan, Chemical Bank, and Manufacturers Hanover, to offer financial backing to the black-owned firm. The federal government and the Noel Fund, which was backed by some of the most successful millionaires on Wall Street, also put up capital.

Jerry was able to get considerable news coverage for the launch of Daniels & Bell, culminating with a story by Terry Robards in the *New York Times* on June 16, 1971, which touted the firm's arrival with a large picture of the two principals and the inside story of what the piece called "the creation of a brokerage firm that probably will become the first black-operated member house of the New York Stock Exchange."

After that coverage, Jerry was able to get a huge crowd to the Stock Exchange eight days later for a news conference that celebrated the firm's successful arrival on the street of dreams. A picture taken by a *New York Post* photographer that day – June 24, 1971 – shows a throng of TV, radio and newspaper reporters eager to meet the two young black entrepreneurs, with a beaming Jerry standing off to the side. Jerry's subsequent news release hailed the development as a victory for what Daniels called "black capitalism." Added Daniels:

"Initially, the uniqueness of our organization should serve as a door opener for at least a token amount of business, particularly among institutions with social consciousness. In the long run, however, the success of Daniels & Bell will depend on service and performance, not the color of our skins and rhetoric." Also attending the press conference was Dan W. Lufkin, the chairman of Donaldson, Lufkin & Jenrette and a then-member of the Board of Governors of the New York Stock Exchange, who called it "an important milestone in Wall Street history. He said "the business community will be well-served by this exciting new firm."

The successful launch allowed Daniels & Bell to become a fixture on Wall Street throughout the 1970s and 1980s, using its position to help finance other black-owned businesses – not just in the United States but in the developing world – that had been overlooked by the vast universe of white-owned firms. In a 1982 profile of Daniels & Bell that hailed the firm as "an empire in black business" stretching from Brooklyn to Africa, the *New York Times* said Bell and his 15 employees were handling large institutional accounts such as Exxon and General Electric but Bell seemed most proud about his work in launching new black-owned businesses. "We've probably underwritten as many black companies as the Small Business Administration, but with private capital instead," Bell told the newspaper, speaking from his 49th-floor office that was brimming with African art, with an expansive view of New York Harbor.

If Jerry's PR clients showed off the trappings of success, so did their promoter. No decade would change him or his family more than the looming 1970s.

Chapter 4: Barcelona Nights

The early years of the 1970s would be defined by the salty sea air on two continents. The saga actually starts at the end of the 1960s, when Jerry Sherman Associates was doing well enough for the family to purchase a summer home on the relatively chic environs of Fire Island, the car-free, ferry-accessible barrier island off central Long Island that was a memorable haven for those who could wrangle access. Fire Island had been saved from overdevelopment in 1964 when residents fought back efforts from legendary master builder Robert Moses to extend the Ocean Parkway and convinced Washington to declare the island a national seashore. That launched a golden era on Fire Island – best remembered for the large gay community centered on Fire Island Pines at the dawn of the LGBTQ liberation movement, but still a family-oriented resort elsewhere – and the Shermans had a front-row seat (well, almost a front row seat) for the heyday of this summer paradise.

Raising the Stakes

It was 1969 when the Shermans rented a house for the summer in the tiny, 80-house community with the delightful name of Lonelyville, on the far west end of Fire Island. They shared the house that first year with Steve Von Molnar and his family. Lonelyville reveled in its isolation – many of the vacation bungalows could only be reached by trekking across the sandy yards of the neighbors – and its most famous residents, the comedian Mel Brooks and his actress wife Anne Bancroft, not far removed from her iconic role as "Mrs. Robinson" in 1967's *The Graduate*.

Just like the Shermans, Brooks and Bancroft – who held onto to their unique home, which had been designed by renowned architect Richard Meier on a passageway called No Name Walk in off-the-beaten track Lonelyville – had incredibly fond memories of Fire Island, where Brooks was working in those years on what would become the classic film *Blazing Saddles*. Years later, Bancroft told the Lonely Planet website that Lonelyville was her favorite place in the world – so it's almost comical to report that the Brooks-Bancroft family and the Shermans didn't exactly get along.

Maybe the oddball Brooks – who apparently can be quirky in real life, just like his film roles – didn't exactly mesh with the fastidious Jerry Sherman. Years later, Bobbi and Emily laughed in recalling that the arrival of a newborn baby – possibly the comedian's son Max, who came in 1972 – set Jerry off. It just annoyed Jerry whenever Brooks came out and walked the baby around and around his home's wrap-around deck – probably to lull the newborn to sleep. "What the hell's wrong with that guy?" Jerry would exclaim as the comic genius behind *The Producers* and his crying infant kept coming around. "Those people are crazy!"

Another time, Jerry – always the PR man – went to the local papers to complain about the lack of easy access to homes like his, which he argued would make it impossible for firefighters to arrive in case of emergency. But Jerry's media campaign also called attention to the fact that Brooks and Bancroft lived in Lonelyville, which – legend has it – angered the comedian. Ironically, in Brooks' 1976 classic film *Silent Movie*, the villains are an evil conglomerate seeking to take over a film studio called Engulf and Devour. That was a thinly disguised jab at

Gulf + Western, the firm where Jerry would be working by the end of the decade. It was just a coincidence – but just another reminder that Jerry was just never meant to hit it off with Mel Brooks.

Like the morning fog rolling off the Atlantic, the Shermans' years on Fire Island are shrouded in a certain amount of myth. Jerry's associates from the Gulf + Western days told the story that while his summer home in Lonelyville was initially two rows back from the oceanfront, a severe storm wiped out some properties, and now Jerry was just one row back from the dunes. One more storm, he told friends, and he'd be able to sell his now-beachfront home for a huge profit. The legend is that's what he did – although Bobbi insists the tale is apocryphal. What is true, according to Bobbi and Emily, is that on the very last day of the summer of '69, as his family sat on the beach reminiscing about what a good time they'd had, Jerry disappeared for a bit, came back and declared that he'd bought the house – just like that! "He was impulsive like that!" Emily recalled with a laugh.

Buying the house in Lonelyville meant three or four more summers of indelible memories. For Emily, nothing beats the time in the early 1970s when Jerry realized that he'd worked too late on a Friday to catch the last ferry, and so on another impulse he decided to rent a seaplane that could take him directly from New York City to the beach. When he arrived, a crowd of people including Bobbi, Emily, and David and their neighbors watched the silver bird descend from the sky and skim the waves – but Jerry may not have thought the whole scheme through.

"They opened the sea plane door – and he's in this business suit," Emily recalled. How would he navigate the patch of water between the plane and the beach? "He rolled up his pants legs, and he beckoned for Bobbi to come out, and she gets him on her back and carries him in. She was proud of her physical prowess."

Home ownership also allowed Bobbi and Jerry to decorate the cottage in their own way – and they didn't disappoint. "They hired a crazy artist who made the house look like a cave, like a psychedelic light show," Emily recalled. Even in the wild, anything-goes ethos of Fire Island in the early 1970s, the wacky makeover was a bit much for some neighbors. "I remember it was an issue," Emily said, "People thought we must be doing drugs because it was such a hippie enclave."

The comfortable, successful life that the Shermans had carved out in Manhattan and on Fire Island in the early 1970s makes what came next a little shocking: A decision to chuck everything abruptly and move to Barcelona, Spain – a city where Jerry and Bobbi had no real business connections and only vague ideas about how the family would support itself. The decision doesn't seem quite so strange for anyone who remembers what American life was like in the early 1970s, when citizens were exhausted from the non-stop turmoil of the last decade, and the overwhelming re-election of Richard Nixon was particularly discouraging for liberals; much like the Lost Generation that flooded Paris during the ennui years after World War I, Europe beckoned in the 1970s for those who were fed up with the repression and culture wars of Richard Nixon's America.

In 1973, Jerry was 43 – right at that mid-life career crossroads faced by many a professional who wonders if he really wants to carry a leather briefcase for the rest of working life. The switch from journalism to public relations had certainly been a lucrative one, but apparently he harbored some dreams of returning to writing, or at least trying something radically different. It was the dawn of the years that writer Tom Wolfe would later brand as "the Me Decade," when it was suddenly in vogue for a Man in a Grey Flannel Suit to start thinking more seriously about self-fulfillment. Recalled Bobbi: "We'd always had dreams of living abroad and that he would write a book – that was the fantasy that he had."

The Spain adventure actually started around 1972 – when Jerry had a business engagement that involved a trip to the Iberian Peninsula. He asked the rest of his family to join him for a Spanish vacation after his meeting – even though Bobbi (as was not uncommon in those days) was afraid of flying. Instead, she brought Emily and David across the Atlantic on an Italian ocean liner, the *Michelangelo*. (Years later, Emily would give Jerry's grandson Arlo the middle name of Michelangelo – perhaps a case of subliminal advertising.) The foursome had a great 10-day vacation –

mostly in the region around the capital city of Madrid – and then Bobbi and the kids got on the boat for the long voyage back to New York.

But a seed had been planted. "Your dad and I loved that Spain trip," Emily remembers Bobbi telling the kids that school year, as the family seriously thought about packing everything up and abruptly moving to Europe.

Ironically, in fleeing New York City for Spain, the Shermans would be leaving the abuses of the Nixon Watergate years to live under an actual fascist, Generalissimo Francisco Franco, who was nearing the end of his life and his roughly four-decade iron grip on Spain as those early years of the 1970s progressed. The long run of authoritarian rule had actually been a boon to the Spanish economy in the 1960s and '70s, especially because the nation experienced less labor unrest than its European neighbors. But Spain was still a nation on edge in those years; college students, who were in a rebellious mode all over the world, clashed bitterly with Franco's security forces in the late 1960s and early 1970s. And the constant presence of the dictator's *Guardia Civil* in the Spanish countryside and his *Policia Armada* in the large cities – uniformed military police who were there to maintain social control – raised the stakes for anyone who was even thinking about criticizing the aging dictator.

The strange part is that – even for liberal parents like Bobbi and Jerry – the strict controls of Franco-era Spain were what may have been most appealing about the move. New York City was hanging by a thread in the early 1970s – an almost unthinkable hellscape of rising murder rates, heroin addiction, burning and abandoned tenement slums, and subway cars covered wall-to-wall in graffiti and wracked by crime. And Emily and David were on the brink of adolescence – the years when they'd face greater exposure to the risks in a decaying city.

"It was a child-friendly culture," Emily recalled of Spain. "They loved children, and there was also 100 percent employment. They had people cleaning the streets, and there was zero crime – because the *Guardia Civil* was patrolling things so tightly."

But the fear and loathing of American society in the early 1970s – especially with Nixon's 1972 re-election and then the increasingly appalling revelations of the president's assorted scandals – were almost certainly on the couple's mind as well. "Watergate was going on and there was a complete disgust with that," Bobbi recalled.

Still, when it came to impulsive decisions, the Fire Island house and the seaplane had nothing on the move to Spain. While they were weighing the move, a New York friend told Bobbi that the seaside city of Barcelona was the best place to live, so the Shermans set their sights on the Catalan capital. (Of course, Barcelona had also been the heart of the region that had fought most fiercely against Franco during the Spanish Civil War, so it had long been a target of the dictator's enmity.) That the family hadn't even seen Barcelona during that initial scouting visit didn't seem an issue. Luckily, their Manhattan friend had shown outstanding taste in recommending one of the world's most irresistible cities. Said Bobbi later: "We were so nervous because we didn't have a place to be. We didn't know anything but we went and it worked out."

They sold their home in Greenwich Village and all of their furniture – pretty much everything except the beloved house on Fire Island – and took the boat back across the Atlantic in 1973. Spain was both an adventure and a challenge. Jerry found the prickly Spanish authorities placed limits on what kind of work he could do, but eventually he did get permission to work as a journalist. Unfortunately for Jerry, he never fulfilled his dream of writing a book, but he did achieve another cherished goal for many a writer by becoming a full-fledged foreign correspondent. Covering events in both Spain and Portugal for his former employer, the *Journal of Commerce*, and other publications such as the *International Herald Tribune*, according to family members, Jerry eked out enough money to keep the family afloat in Barcelona – even if the income was nothing like the salad days of the late 1960s and early 1970s.

But working as a journalist posed a different risk for the Shermans' stay in Spain – the risk that Jerry's reporting might offend Franco at the end of his four decades in power. Once, Jerry filed a piece for a widely read international publication that he felt had been sharply critical of the military strongman in Madrid. He was certain he'd crossed an invisible line, and he braced his family for the worst. "He thought, this is it – Franco is going to get really mad and we'll have to leave and we thought that was like a badge of honor," Bobbi recalled. But they'd misjudged the dictator's reaction. Instead, Franco reprinted the article in several newspapers.

Knowing few people in and around Barcelona, Jerry made new connections nonetheless. A friend suggested that Jerry tried to contact a man named Larry Wald, a film producer, who lived down the Mediterranean coastline – so they drove down and slipped a note under his door. Much to Bobbi and Jerri's surprise, Wald called them back and soon he and Jerry became fast friends, nearly working together on what could have been the project of a lifetime a few years later.

Spain was every bit the mid-life adventure the Shermans had been looking for – and yet the family knew it wouldn't last. One day in August 1974, the family took a trip to see Venice, and they were walking past a newsstand when they saw the headline: "Nixon resigns." Bobbi and Jerry turned to each other to voice the same thought. "I guess we can go home now." The truth was a little more complicated. The Shermans were, not surprisingly, beginning to run out of money.

When the family returned to New York City in 1974, they were essentially starting from scratch all over again "When we left Spain we took a ship," Emily recalled. "Dad had about $350 in cash and the house on Fire Island. We went to our friends the Coopermans, and we slept on the floor of their house for a week, maybe 10 days." During that time, Jerry was going out every day hustling to find the next new thing.

Not surprisingly, it was the old connections that pulled him through. Jerry's old friend Travers Bell, whom Jerry had helped to launch on Wall Street, was now suddenly in a position to repay him. One of Daniels & Bell's investments in the mid-1970s was a candy factory in one of the most rundown sections of Brooklyn, which was plagued by arson and urban decay throughout the decade. Of course, Jerry actually knew something about the candy industry, having once covered it as a journalist, so when Bell asked him to help run the plant, he jumped at the opportunity. "We would get these boxes of candy when he came home," Emily recalled.

It was enough money to at least start to rebuild their old life in Manhattan. Soon, the Shermans rented an apartment on 14th Street near the edge of Greenwich Village, not far from where the family used to live and the private school that Emily and David had attended before Spain. The apartment was small – just two bedrooms that were handed over to the kids, while Bobbi and Jerry slept in the living room – but at least it was a beachhead.

Looking to get back into the public relations game, Jerry called in a chit with another old friend, Mike Candell. Candell was working out of West 56th Street – just a block from where he and Jerry had been during the 1960s – and now it was Candell who had some empty office space that Jerry could use as he hustled for new work. "Mike gave him an office and he scrounged up one client and started rebuilding his business," Emily recalled. But times had changed. The

Raising the Stakes

U.S. economy was in the midst of a sustained rough patch in the mid-to-late '70s – and the industrial clients that Jerry had written about in the '50s and publicized in the '60s were generally the hardest hit.

Nonetheless, Jerry ploughed forward to open Jerry Sherman/Marketing Services at 120 East 56th Street, specializing in public, corporate, and investor relations. But there was also a new twist, as he looked to work with Bobbi on a new venture that targeted the field of industrial films – with dreams of an occasional detour into theatrical drama.

B.J. Films (which stood for Bobbi and Jerry, obviously) was announced in a press release on May 19, 1977, with Bobbi as the new venture's president. The primary goal was "to conceive, develop, produce and market motion pictures – film and videotape – in at least four different areas: Corporate, industrial, sales training and public service." The couple also partnered with Marvin Rothenberg, a well-known director of industrial and commercial films.

What survives of B.J. Films showed that Bobbi and Jerry largely pursued the more lucrative – if less exciting – big-business clients such as the Cleveland-based Tenna Corporation, which made electric motors and radio parts. "The Tenna Story is one which lends itself dynamically to the persuasive, dramatic medium of film," Bobbi wrote to a company executive in the spring of 1977. "From the Company's one-antenna beginning in the competitive post-war era of 1945 to its present multi-product position as one of the major-manufacturer marketers of automotive accessories, there is a tale of growth and excellence that can be graphically illustrated by the art and the craft of a well-conceived, well-executed motion picture." Other paperwork pushes a plan for a 25-minute public-service film called "How To Retire...And Start Living" that was to be funded by large financial services and travel and leisure firms with a proposed budget of $100,000.

The proposed workload of B.J. Films was potentially lucrative but for the most part not particularly sexy, in contrast to the other known would-be project for the young movie company: A bold scheme to work with heavyweight boxing champion Muhammad Ali – who was still the title holder in 1977, as his long and brilliant career began to wind down – and screen icon Diahann Carroll (like Jerry, a Bronx native) on a pirate movie that would be filmed on Spain's Gold Coast. Jerry even held onto newspaper clippings from Spanish newspapers that excitedly reported on the possibility that the world's most famous athlete might be coming to film there, and the articles even included a photo of Jerry and a colleague scouting locations.

Unfortunately, those handfuls of newspaper clippings are all that ever really came of the project. Today, Bobbi doesn't even remember that much of the venture other than it was an unrealized pipe dream tied to their friend back in Spain, Larry Wald. Indeed, the various business ventures of Bobbi and Jerry Sherman in the late 1970s masked a broader reality. The New York that the family returned to was different from the one they had left for Spain. The American economy in the late 1970s was terrible, with skyrocketing gasoline prices, long lines at the pump, and something called "stagflation" – a macroeconomic malady that caused prices to continue rising and interest rates to hit record levels even as unemployment was also on the increase. To many experts – as memorialized in the phrase "Ladies and Gentlemen, the Bronx is Burning," the title of a popular book and ESPN mini-series – 1977 was the year that New York City hit the nadir of its decline, with hundreds of arson fires devouring abandoned buildings from the Bronx to Bushwick, and massive looting in July of that year when a citywide blackout struck.

For close to two decades, Jerry has been his own man in the PR world, but after several sluggish years, and with college for Emily and David on the not-too-distant horizon, he began to consider other options. Suddenly, the corporate world didn't look so bad.

Chapter 5: The Toughest PR Job in America

It was another moment of great change for Jerry Sherman, and once again his longtime friend Myron Candell was right in the middle of it. It was Candell who – thanks to all his contacts in the Manhattan business world – urged Jerry to apply for the kind of job that the now 48-year-old had always avoided: Corporate public relations. Candell successfully encouraged Jerry to seek the job as top PR executive at one of the world's largest conglomerates, Gulf + Western.

Bobbi recalled that "things weren't going so great" for Jerry when the Gulf + Western position was proposed and that Candell has to lobby both Jerry and the company for the deal to happen, The idea seemed like a real whipsaw from the free-spirited escape to Barcelona just a few short years earlier. Even as a teenager, Emily picked up on the tension.

"I remember the interview process – it was a big deal to have even more than one (interview) and [my parents] were discussing it at the table, and he was expressing some concern over going to work for a large corporation," Emily recalled. "I seem to remember an expression of – 'That's like working for the man.'"

There was good reason to be concerned.

It's been several decades now since the Gulf + Western nameplate flew over Manhattan from its hulking silver-and-black 44-story headquarters that towered over the southwestern corner of Central Park, at Columbus Circle. For anyone under the age of 45 or so, it may be hard to convey how the company came to symbolize the vast American industrial conglomerate of the 1960s and '70s. Which explains why Mel Brooks was able to get cheap laughs by naming a fictional company "Engulf and Devour." The joke rang true because when Jerry interviewed for the job at Gulf + Western around 1978, the company had engulfed and devoured dozens of smaller businesses, from auto parts suppliers to a major Hollywood studio to two of Jerry's beloved sports teams, the New York Knicks and the New York Rangers.

Raising the Stakes

No one quite understood it at the time, but the type of conglomerate epitomized by Gulf + Western was an evolutionary stage of American capitalism. Ever since the dawn of the Industrial Revolution, companies that made both raw products such as steel, or consumer goods such as automobiles, were subject to the scourge of the business cycle; investors would reap the rewards during the boom years, only to suffer devastating losses in the inevitable downturn, from the Panic of 1893 to the mother of all financial crises, the Great Depression of the 1930s. But not all businesses were on that same cycle; the movie business, for example, prospered during the depths of the Depression, as Americans looked for matinee escapism from the bad times. From that reality sprung an idea: What if investors could buy stock in a large corporation that owned a basket of industries in different sectors, to even out stock returns amid the vagaries of the business cycle. And that idea had its champion in Charles Bluhdorn, the colorful founder of Gulf + Western Industries, Inc.

Dubbed a "romantic businessman" by no less an expert than studio icon Barry Diller, Bluhdorn was a true product of the

20th Century – not unlike his future PR man, Jerry Sherman. He'd been born in 1926 in Vienna – and his fairly prosperous family fled the region in 1938 as the terrors of Nazism were on the rise, motivated by the Jewish ancestry of Bluhdorn's mother. The World War II years were a blur for the Bluhdorns – the teenager then still known by his birth name of Karl made it to London, where he continued his schooling while his parents barely escaped Hitler's advance on France, fleeing to New York in 1940. When Bluhdorn crossed the Atlantic two years later, half the ships in his convoy were sunk by German U-boats. It was the first of many close calls.

Despite the thick and often incomprehensible Austrian accent that he retained for the rest of his life, the refugee who re-invented himself as Charlie Bluhdorn was quick to adopt the ways of his new homeland – jumpstarted by a stint in the U.S. Air Force that sent him to Mississippi as World War II wound down. Back in New York, Bluhdorn took night classes at Columbia but got his best education from a book called *Security Analysis*, which unlocked the secrets of

Raising the Stakes

trading. Betting big on malt and coffee futures, Bluhdorn had made his first million by the time he was 21. The biggest lesson that he learned, though, was the art of buying low and selling high. In 1956, the year he turned 30, Bluhdorn led a group of investors that bought an especially unpromising company for the bargain basement price of just $1 million. The company, Michigan Plating & Stamping, had made rear bumpers for the soon-to-be-defunct Studebakers. But somehow, it became the launching pad for a global business empire. When Bluhdorn added another small auto-parts firm in Texas two years later, he decided to brand the company as Gulf (for the location of the Texas affiliate) + Western (for Michigan, which seemed to be out West from Bluhdorn's perspective). Somehow, the name seemed to reflect the broad ambitions that Bluhdorn spent the next two decades fulfilling.

The humble auto-parts business sent Bluhdorn into an orbit in which he would do deals with the Vatican and Fidel Castro and, according to a posthumous profile by Robert Sam Anson in *Vanity Fair,* even turned up on Richard Nixon's White House tapes as someone "to be bled for a quarter of a million dollars." Indeed, if you'd pitched Bluhdorn's life story as a possible movie to Paramount – the struggling studio that he and Gulf + Western purchased in 1966, and then took to the top with hits such as *Love Story* and *The Godfather* – no one would have believed it. The list of business ventures that Gulf + Western would engulf and devour included defense contractors, supermarket chains, a lucrative venture called New Jersey Zinc, sugar plantations that crisscrossed a wide swath of what would become Bluhdorn's island hideaway retreat in the Dominican Republic, the publishing giant Simon & Schuster, Madison Square Garden including its franchises the Knicks and Rangers, and Paramount, which was the crown jewel. Gulf + Western even bought the legendary Memphis-based Stax Records during the heyday of American soul music in 1968, and it also purchased the library of the Desilu Studios, which includes "Star Trek" as well as the classic episodes of "I Love Lucy" with the studio's founders Lucille Ball and Desi Arnez. Gulf + Western even owned the Japanese video maker Sega, a key player in the arcade gaming boom of the 1970s and '80s. When Warren Beatty picked up the Academy Award for *Reds* in 1982, he name-checked the Manhattan billionaire behind the studio. "I want to name . . . Charles Bluhdorn, who owns Gulf + Western and God knows what else," said Beatty, "no matter how much we might have liked to strangle each other from time to time."

Over time, Bluhdorn's blustery personality and his iconoclastic business practices became the stuff of legend; very few other businessmen could inspire profiles in both *Vanity Fair* and *The New Yorker* that appeared many years after his death and disappearance from the stage.

"In the '60s and 70s, 'conglomerate' suggested a corporation whose only purpose was to maintain a dizzying rate of growth, which it did by the constant acquisition of other companies," Michael Korda wrote in *The New Yorker* in 1996. "By reputation, Charles G. Bluhdorn was the most ruthless conglomerateur of them all. His violent temper and many eccentricities made him a celebrity." While he was alive, *Life* magazine had dubbed Bluhdorn "the Mad Austrian."

Raising the Stakes

Marty Shea, who joined the PR shop at Gulf + Western not long before Jerry began working there, still marvels at the audaciousness of Bluhdorn's rise in the 1950s and '60s, and how his idea for cornering the essentially but unsexy market for auto parts somehow evolved into a scheme to takeover Hollywood. Bluhdorn, Shea recalled, "created an atmosphere where everybody was running wild" buying up properties. In the 1960s, it was becoming conventional wisdom that the rise of television had damaged the movie business and that a studio could be purchased on the cheap. "He thought that a winner could be Hollywood."

"You know my hobby is business, right?" Bluhdorn once told a reporter from *Forbes*. "I eat, sleep, dream the business. I get my best ideas at 4 o'clock in the morning." A separate anecdote from the *Economist*: "He enjoyed nothing more than tough haggling, as he tried first to cajole and then to bully an adversary into a deal, but he also had a rich vein of Viennese schmaltz in his make-up. When a board meeting in 1969 to discuss selling the Paramount production studio was interrupted by the accidental death of the pet poodle of the actress Miss Ali McGraw, Bluhdorn set off for a poodle farm 80 miles away to fetch Miss McGraw a replacement. The sale of the studio was never discussed again."

If it all sounds like a financial fairy tale from a different world, it was. By the late 1970s some financial experts were already starting to question the wisdom of one company trying to manage so many different industries instead of focusing on leadership in one core area. Indeed, some Wall Street gurus were looking at a more efficient way to accomplish what Bluhdorn and his lesser rivals had achieved in the 1960s with the rise of the conglomerate. In 1976, a little known firm named Vanguard had launched its "Vanguard Index 500 Fund," which allowed investors to hedge their bets across the entire stock market. It's not a coincidence that the dawn of the mutual funds coincided with the peak years of the company, the mid-to-late 1970s, when moviegoers were chuckling at the "Engulf & Devour" dig in *Silent Movie*.

That wasn't apparent when Jerry began interviewing for the job at Gulf + Western in 1978 – that the next 15 years would be spent more in a selling rather than buying mode. And while Jerry's worries about working for "the Man" in midtown Manhattan were legitimate fears, the job running PR for the conglomerate posed other potential problems. Gulf + Western, in the mid-1970s, was notorious for chewing up its public relations staff and spitting them out. And the culprit was not so much the occasionally volcanic Bluhdorn as the man that the Gulf + Western CEO had entrusted with all PR and marketing work, a former Paramount executive named Martin Davis.

"Jerry's job was the worst job in America," Bobbi recalled with a laugh decades later – and this was hardly a wife's hyperbole. Right around the time that Jerry accepted the job offer, *Fortune* magazine published a lengthy article that spelled out in chapter and verse exactly how difficult it was to work in the pressure-cooker PR shop at Gulf + Western. In fact, the headline couldn't have been more clear: "Why P.R. Men Don't Last Long at Gulf + Western." The opening paragraph of the story by writer Donald D. Holt does suggests, however, why

Jerry would have been interested in the position.

"The top public-relations job at Gulf + Western Industries sounds like the kind a fellow would do anything to keep," it begins. "The salary is above average in the p.r. world – ranging up to around $80,000. The big corner office that goes with the job has majestic views of New York's Central Park and the Hudson River. Among the other perks are access to company-leased luxury cars, good seats for Knicks and Rangers games at Madison Square Garden (which G. + W. owns), and private screens of movies from Paramount Pictures (which G. + W. also owns). When winter comes, there are company-owned sugar operations and hotels in the Dominican Republic that an enterprising public-relations executive can find an excuse to check out."

So far so good, right? But then the articles goes on to mention that a revolving door of at least seven or eight people – including one man who'd quit, come back and left again – had held the top PR post at Gulf + Western in less than a decade. And that didn't even include the short stays of their underlings; the article quips that "Gulf

+ Western's revolving door had spun so fast that veterans joke about having a reunion at Yankee Stadium." Clearly the problem started at the top with the mercurial Bluhdorn, who is described as "notoriously touchy" about the press that he received. The *Fortune* article quotes one former company vice president: "With Charlie, there is no such thing as a balanced story. If it isn't 100 percent for him, it is 100 percent against him."

But the story also notes that the PR officers didn't have much direct contact with Bluhdorn. Instead, the day-to-day tone of the job was set by Davis, the Bronx-born movie industry veteran whom Bluhdorn had imported from Hollywood to oversee Gulf + Western's image-making machinery, including marketing and PR. *Fortune*'s Holt described Davis as "a tough taskmaster" who earned some respect from some associates for his 12-hour-a-day work ethic and fairness, but who was described bitterly – and for the most part anonymously – by some of the former executives who were now outside the revolving door. Here is a particularly devastating passage from the article:

Raising the Stakes

One thing that Davis-watchers agree on is that he uses intimidation as a management technique. "I never heard Davis actually talk," says one former underling; he and others say that Davis was given to screaming – particularly on the telephone. And he kept subordinates off-balance with such tricks as letting them stand, unacknowledged, in front of his desk for long minutes as he scribbled away, head down, on the papers before him. However he did it, he managed to create an atmosphere so charged that the three words, "Marty wants it," could set off pandemonium in the public-relations department.

One former executive recalls that he couldn't leave the office in the evening until Davis's secretary had phoned to relay the boss's benediction. Sometimes no call would come, and as dusk settled on Central Park thirty-four floors below his massive windows, the bewildered subordinate would call Davis's office himself, only to be told Davis had left a half-hour earlier, having forgotten to order the liberating phone call.

Andrew Nelson, the man who came from Singer [the sewing-machine company] freely admits he found the climate intimidating. "I would sit in Davis' office in my $300 suit and feel like a child," Nelson says. "Outside that office, I was powerful; inside I was nothing. I was scared of him. I would go out of there almost crawling." That, apparently, was the last thing Davis wanted. One colleague from movie days, Hy Smith, who is now a vice president of United Artists, insists that Davis never liked subordinates who seemed to be afraid of him. "Some people would walk into his office and sweat," says Smith. "They didn't last long."

In short, it didn't sound like the easiest path for Jerry to get back to the top of the PR world – but that wasn't all. The *Fortune* article notes that the office was rife with rumors – all of them unconfirmed – that Gulf + Western executives had their telephones tapped, or were surveilled after-hours, or were the subject of extensive background checks. The magazine did note that Davis had admitted that in the early 1970s a private investigator had sifted through the desktops and trashcans in an effort to learn the source of "persistent leaks" to the news media. What's more, the main mission of the PR department – to sell a positive image of Gulf + Western through the media – had become difficult if not impossible; Wall Street skepticism about Bluhdorn and his strategy had begun to settle in, and it was known that the U.S. Securities and Exchange Commission had been conducting an investigation of the corporation and its high-flying CEO. Still, the most devastating passage in the article may have been the author's interview with Nelson, the former Singer executive, who had abandoned his upscale career in corporate communications to work in a series of low-paying editing jobs at small newspapers. "'I'm happy,' he says, nursing a Heineken in a local Elks club in Connecticut. 'You can tell Marty that I'm not scared anymore. And that means an awful lot.'"

Years later, those who worked under Davis at Gulf + Western would not quibble with the basic premise of the article. Marty Shea noted that he'd worked for some notoriously demanding bosses in the media business – including Sumner Redstone at Viacom and Les Moonves at CBS – but it was Davis who was "over the top," especially in his obsessive attention to detail.

"If he was hosting a dinner -- whether it be 400 people or four people – he'd want to see the seating arrangement at that table or all the tables before anybody even entered the room," Shea recalled. "He was meticulous – he would go over the list and make sure everybody was seated where he wanted them." Likewise, Shea recalled, Davis had strong opinions about where people stayed in hotels during meetings out-of-town. "He'd say, 'I'm going to be on the 12th floor so I don't want this guy above the 5th floor' – on different elevator banks, even."

And yet despite the doom and gloom of the *Fortune* article, it was hard to imagine Jerry meeting a similar fate at Gulf + Western. Instead, he seemed to be uniquely designed for the demanding job specifications. The biggest reason was Jerry's unnatural self-confidence – the thing that had allowed him to start a newspaper career at age 16, ditch his successful PR business for a two-year adventure in Spain, and win Bobbi back after she had just married someone else. It also had helped that he had an ability not to let the heated give-and-take of the volatile workplace stick to him; often, he gave back as good as he got whenever the volume was raised. What's more, Davis had been raised on the humble streets of the Bronx – just like Jerry – and he was able to relate to his high-pressure boss in a way that many of the Ivy League types in the corporate workplace could not. And thanks to his networking through the New York Financial Writers Association and his long experience in the battlefield of financial journalism, he had better connections than most of his predecessors at Gulf + Western.

"I don't think anything could have prepared him for how psycho the dynamic was with Bluhdorn," Bobbi conceded. Yet Jerry – despite the notorious reputation of Gulf + Western – approached the job with confidence and also a kind of a strait-laced sense that if he played by the rules, things would work out for him.

"I think he felt so solid in his sense of right and wrong that it enabled him to be strong with these guys when he needed to be," Bobbi recalled. "He could also be so charming that I think he was able to soften the blows. And with his connections in the press he had built up – people respected him. So that helped him put some fires out."

Indeed, Emily – who was at height of the rebellious teenager years when her dad accepted the position at Gulf + Western – said she was stunned and a little taken aback by how quickly that Jerry had transformed from his ex-pat-in-Spain persona of the early 1970s into a defender of this large American conglomerate.

"I was like, 'Where did that guy go? – because then you couldn't say something critical about Gulf + Western at the dinner table," Emily recalled many years later with a sense of wonder. "I knew it was going to be serious! He drank the Kool-Aid, hook line and sinker, and he took his job defending the honor of the corporation and these crazy moguls at the top very seriously – there would be no PR that was negative about them, even at his own dinner table!"

Raising the Stakes

Jerry took his job seriously in those early years because he had to. Reporters were constantly calling about the SEC probe or other potentially negative stories about the company. Meanwhile, Jerry's arrival in 1978 coincided with the moment that Gulf + Western was abruptly shifting gears, ending the era of rapid expansion and instead looking to unload the less profitable and less well managed divisions of the firm. Many of the press releases that Jerry penned in those early years, when Bluhdorn was still the CEO of the company, were to announce that Gulf + Western was selling off yet another asset.

The same year that Jerry joined the company, Gulf + Western had paid an unprecedented sum of money – some $3.3 million – to print its annual report in *Time* magazine, hoping the wide circulation would stir investor interest and boost the corporation's sagging stock price. It didn't. In fact, a year later a major story in *Forbes* insisted that Gulf + Western had what it called "a $400 million credibility gap" – meaning that an extensive analysis of the firm's assets showed its value might be $400 million higher under different management – because Wall Street investors simply didn't trust Bluhdorn. This despite that fact that the SEC investigations of the firm that had caused so much fear and loathing in the financial media ultimately proved to be inconsequential.

Indeed, Jerry's first appearance in the Associated Press as the company spokesman came on August 15, 1979, when he confirmed that Gulf + Western had been under investigation by the SEC for more than three years. He said the Dominican operations of the company had been conducted with "honor and integrity," and that "we welcome any inquiry into our activities by the Dominican government." That probe, which looked at possible tax violations and labor abuses with the firm's operations in the Dominican Republic, resulted in the company agreeing to spend $39 million in the island nation; the second, which looked at more serious allegations of pension fund abuse, ended without Bluhdorn or the company having to make any restitution at all.

Still, Jerry learned that a critical part of his job was cleaning up after Bluhdorn's occasional eruptions or misstatements. His efforts to straighten out one mess that occurred at Gulf + Western's annual meeting at the Felt Forum, the theater within the bowels of its Madison Square Garden, would become legendary among his colleagues. Bluhdorn – not known for his political correctness – went on a tangent about business prospects in Japan which led to his referring to the people there as "Nippies," stunning those in attendance, including some of Manhattan's top financial journalists. Jerry worked the phones, called in his chits with the writers, and somehow convinced them that "Nippies" was merely a Bluhdorn term of endearment. Amazingly, he managed to keep the embarrassing incident out of the papers.

On June 5, 1980, Jerry orchestrated a press event that company officials hoped would be a game-changer for Gulf + Western, not to mention the future of American transportation. Before a throng of reporters, company officials drove two vehicles – a VW Rabbit and a large van – noiselessly around Columbus Circle to show off fully electric engines that had been developed by the company's engineers. The firm had been working on a zinc-chloride battery to power the device since 1972 and now planned to open a pilot production facility in North Carolina. The previous year had brought a huge spike in gasoline prices and long lines at the pump because of the Iranian hostage crisis, and so any plan to reduce America's dependence on foreign oil was greeted with considerable excitement.

The president of Gulf + Western – Jim Judelson, a low-key engineer who often took a backseat to the bombastic Bluhdorn and Davis – did not try to curb his enthusiasm. "We at Gulf + Western consider this to be a major achievement in the world of high technology – perhaps one of the most meaningful developments since the turn of the century, with important ecological, economic and political ramifications," he said. Alas, it did not live up to the hype. By the year's end, the U.S. Department of Energy was reporting that the battery life was not meeting the projections and that only highly trained personnel could recharge it. The electric car would eventually become a reality on America's highways, but long after Gulf + Western was gone.

Charlie Bluhdorn was not a particularly old man – only four years older than Jerry, in fact – and given the fact that Gulf + Western was his baby, there's every reason to assume that he would have tried to hold the conglomerate together as long as possible. But by the time that Jerry arrived at the Columbus Circle headquarters, Bluhdorn's health was starting to decline. Like many wildly successful businessman, the Gulf + Western founder increasingly spent time on his obsessions – his estate and other interests in the Dominican Republic. According to the posthumous profile in *Vanity Fair*, Bluhdorn spent the last five years of his life spending $30 million to construct a massive artists' colony in the Dominican highlands, with spectacular Riviera-style architecture and a Roman amphitheater seating 5,000 people. But when his friend Frank Sinatra arrived to christen the new arena with a concert, the Gulf + Western CEO was almost too sick to attend. No one in his inner circle, including the top executives back in Manhattan, knew that Bluhdorn was suffering from leukemia. "He hid his illness from nearly everyone, fearing it would be blood for the sharks already sniffing his undervalued stock," Robert Sam Anson wrote. "When he could no longer put off treatment, he said that he was going for a gall-bladder operation."

On February 19, 1983, Bluhdorn boarded his private jet in the Dominican Republic for the familiar flight back to New York. What happened over the Atlantic Ocean that day would change the life of Jerry Sherman – and the people around him – for years to come.

Chapter 6: The Disorderly World of Marty Davis

Family members later reported doctors had warned Gulf + Western founder Charlie Bluhdorn that he was too ill to travel on that fateful day in the winter of 1983 – but he took off anyway. By the time his Gulfsteam jet had landed that Saturday afternoon, Bluhdorn was dead; he was just 56 years old. As Anson notes in his *Vanity Fair* profile, the Gulf + Western CEO's unexpected death launched all sorts of crazy rumors. He wrote that there were whispers that Bluhdorn had "died not aboard his Gulfstream II but in the plush confines of his Dominican estate, then been loaded aboard his plane as if alive, in the manner of El Cid. No, said still another, Charlie had died on the plane, and of a heart attack – experienced while communing intimately with a comely business reporter. There was even a report, which *Variety* checked out, that Charlie had been murdered—the means poison, the poisoner acting on instructions of the Mafia. Hadn't *The Godfather*, after all, been a Paramount release?" The reality was much more routine: That the sickly Bluhdorn, who'd been traveling with his long-time wife Yvette, had died from a myocardial infarction. A heart attack.

But, needless to say, news of Bluhdorn's death triggered something of an earthquake back in the massive steel headquarters on Columbus Circle. After all, the Gulf + Western founder had just gone to great lengths to hide his illness because he thought it would lower the company's stock price; the reality that he was now gone and that the conglomerate faced an unknown transition and an even less certain future was the classic definition of a potential public-relation crisis that would be carefully watched on Wall Street. For Marty Davis, Jerry, and the rest of their crew back in New York, the day that Charlie Bluhdorn died was maybe the most memorable of their career. Davis – the executive who obsessed over dinner-party seating charts – was particularly manic.

"Davis made these guys write the press release over and over and over again," Marty Shea recalled of that day. "I asked Jerry why and he said that he [Davis] didn't like the headline." Not unlike the passing of a supreme leader at the height of the former Soviet Union, the process of announcing Bluhdorn's death became intimately wrapped up in the battle to succeed him. Shea recalls the drama at Columbus Circle that day as "an absolute explosion." And Davis – whose main talent was creating and crafting a message, with the help of lieutenants like Jerry – was showing that, for all his manic energy – he was the man taking charge of the chaotic situation.

It was a test that Jerry seems to have passed with flying colors. The death of the pioneering industrialist was featured in newspapers from coast-to-coast, in obituaries that typically quoted Jerry on the cause of death and tended to emphasize Bluhdorn's successes both in the business world and in philanthropy, while overlooking issues such as Gulf + Western's sagging stock price or the late CEO's notorious temper.

"During Bluhdorn's stewardship, Gulf + Western mushroomed into a giant corporation, a multi-billion-dollar firm with operations divided into seven groups – apparel and home furnishings, automotive replacement parts, consumer and agricultural products, financial services, leisure time, manufacturing, natural resources and building products," noted the first article about Bluhdorn's death, by the United Press International. The piece stressed that Bluhdorn was a trustee of Texas Wesleyan College and Trinity Episcopal Schools Corp. in New York, a member of the board of directors of United Way of Tri-State, and a co-chairman of the New York chapter of the American Cancer Society, the National Multiple Sclerosis Dinner Campaign, and of the United States Savings Bond Drive. It noted that, "The City Club of New York gave Bluhdorn its Distinguished New Yorker Award for his leadership in taking action to fight problems facing Americans in New York and around the country."

It would be nearly a generation before more risqué profiles of Bluhdorn and his high-profile Hollywood deals would be published – coincidentally or not, after Jerry's tenure with the company had ended. Just two days after his death, the billionaire executive was buried in a small private ceremony in Ridgefield, Connecticut, his primary home. The mourning period was a brief one; by the next day, the New York Times was already publishing speculation over who would take over Gulf + Western and its 100,000 employees. But the speculation was mostly wrong.

""The board will get together this week, and the succession that will take place will be orderly," said David N. Judelson, G + W's president," in the *New York Times* article of Feb. 22, 1983. "The board we have put together is an independent one, and is one of the real strengths of this corporation," he added. Analysts named Mr. Judelson as one strong candidate. Other in-house contenders for the job include three executive vice presidents, Martin S. Davis, Lawrence E. Levinson, and James I. Spiegel. Of the three, Mr. Spiegel appeared to have the inside track, an ex-Gulf + Western executive said. "Jim Spiegel was Bluhdorn's wonder boy," he said. David S. Moore, an analyst at Donaldson Lufkin & Jenrette, had a different opinion. "I am not convinced the board will be quick to name anybody," he said. "But when they get around to it, I think they will choose Judelson. He is an extraordinarily competent person, and was a close associate of Mr. Bluhdorn's.'"

The early dismissal of Marty Davis underestimated the former Hollywood executive's ambition and his ability to manipulate opinion. One day later, Davis would be elected the new CEO of Gulf + Western – acing out the engineering-minded, straight-laced Judelson as well as Bluhdorn protégé Spiegel. The move was announced in a press release written by Jerry, quoting his new boss as stating, "The course Mr. Bluhdorn and his senior management charted for Gulf + Western over the past quarter of a century resulted in unprecedented growth, and the long-range programs now being implemented are reshaping Gulf + Western into a company better positioned to not only continue this growth, but to capitalize on new opportunities." Judelson, clearly stung by the realization he'd been leapfrogged by Davis, would leave the company less than a month later. (And the *Times* would act like it saw all of this coming, writing that Davis "has long been viewed as the man who knows more about the company than anyone else and, moreover, one with a good following on Wall Street. He was also 'a good pal of Charley (sic),' one analyst remarked.")

Raising the Stakes

One side-effect of Davis' surprising seizure of Gulf + Western was that it strengthened Jerry's position and his role within the company. He'd been a vice president, reporting directly to Davis, for nearly four years by the time that Bluhdorn died – already having survived far longer than any of his predecessors in the job that *Fortune* had once deemed the toughest in all of PR. He already had a strong working relationship with the new CEO – unlike the other failed candidates, Judelson and Siegel – and the ability to speak freely with his fellow Bronx native Davis that none of his more intimidated colleagues seemed to share.

Vanity Fair would call Davis "the tough streetwise kid from the Bronx who fled a dysfunctional home at 14, rented a room on the Grand Concourse for four dollars a week, and toiled as a delivery boy when he wasn't stealing copies of the *Daily News* and hawking them for two cents apiece."

That said, a close working relationship with Marty Davis was no guarantee of long-term job security for Jerry – only because in February of 1983 it seemed there was no guarantee that Davis – or, more importantly,

Gulf + Western itself – would be in place for very much longer. During the week that Bluhdorn died and Davis became the new CEO, the stock price of Gulf + Western skyrocketed, not because of confidence in the new boss but because Wall Street believed the perpetually undervalued firm and its assets were an easy takeover target.

As Davis was assuming control, UPI was reporting that one of the most notorious "corporate raiders" of the early 1980s, billionaire investor Carl Icahn, had bought some one-to-two-million shares of Gulf + Western stock on the open market and now had a 2.6 percent stake in the company; the wire service noted that sometimes Icahn actually went through with his takeover threats while other targets were forced to find so-called "white knight" investors to buy back Icahn's shares at considerably more than what he had paid for them.

And Icahn wasn't the only one with a seeming interest now that Bluhdorn was out of the picture; another Wall Street player, Carl Linder, the head of Cincinnati-based American Financial Corp., was also buying up G + W stock. The next day, the *New York Times* noted that another notorious trader,

Ivan Boesky – whose aggressive business dealings would later partly inspire the 1980s movie *Wall Street*, was also buying shares of the company. Not surprisingly, this news had caused the price of Gulf + Western stock to skyrocket, increasing is value by $7 a share, or close to 40 percent, by the end of the hectic week.

For Gulf + Western to survive as an entity, Davis would need to accelerate the program that Bluhdorn had actually begun in the late 1970s – to pare down the company, beginning with some of the more capital-intensive and lower-profit operations that had the greatest potential to cut into the conglomerate's bottom line. With Judelson's departure, Davis streamlined the company's management structure, basically eliminating the job of president and vesting more power in the division heads, including the dynamic rising boss of the Paramount Studios-dominated entertainment unit, Barry Diller.

Vanity Fair would, years later, buy into the notion of Davis as Gulf + Western's savior: "While he was Charlie's lieutenant, he was the Elmer's glue," says Don Oresman. "Without him this place would've fallen apart. He worked with the bankers, the lawyers, he did everything. Charlie was crazy and chaotic and brilliant and outrageous and out of control. When Charlie died, Martin inherited an unholy mess, 110,000 employees, every company under the sun. Charlie bought everything. You couldn't even count the businesses. They were all over, Rust Belt crap—everything. It was all crap!"

By August 1983, or just six months after Bluhdorn died, Davis was deep into a complete makeover of Gulf + Western. Wrote *Newsweek*: "Davis is as hard-nosed and as egotistical as his predecessor, but Wall Street seems to think he will bring stability and a more traditional management style to the company." That summer, Davis announced that Gulf + Western would divest itself of 20 percent of its assets, or about $1 billion in sales "We're in a different mode," the new CEO told the *New York Times*. In addition to shedding unprofitable or unwanted divisions from cigars to zinc, Gulf + Western also sold off its large stock portfolio that Bluhdorn – with his trading savvy – had used to bolster the company profits. The new focus would be largely on the entertainment portfolio, consumer goods and finance – with the ultimate goal of a leaner company that would deliver for the shareholders. Explained *Forbes*: "And without speaking ill of the dead, some think that, in some ways, it will change for the better (without Bluhdorn at the helm). 'In the near term,' says one Wall Street analyst, 'the new management team may be less inclined to say the hell with the shareholders.'"

The rapid turn of events on Columbus Circle was unusually dramatic, but it also highlighted a new era that was beginning for American capitalism, for Wall Street, and – most importantly – for the role of public relations. After the gloomy economic downturns of the 1970s, the Dow Jones Industrial Average took off in the early 1980s, in a reflection of the American boosterism and the optimism that was coming from the new president Ronald Reagan down in Washington. Once again, making money was popular – even sexy. Television celebrated "The Lifestyles of the Rich and Famous" while the ethics of the bull market were debated in movies such as *Barbarians at the Gates*, *Other People's*

Raising the Stakes

Money and, of course, *Wall Street*. And a brash egotistical real-estate developer named Donald Trump was about to become a best-selling author.

If you take a step back, you can look at Jerry's now nearly four-decade career in financial journalism and public relations to see how much the business world – and perceptions of the world – had changed since the end of World War II. In the 1940s and '50s, in that booming economy, the focus was straightforward reporting on commodities prices and new products. But in the 1980s, the action had moved from heavy industry to finance. American capitalism had become a clash of big egos – larger-than-life CEOs and dynamic "corporate raiders" whose every move would be tracked and analyzed in a business press that was both much larger and much more influential than when Jerry had started out as a copy boy at the *Journal of Commerce*. That was the sea that Gulf + Western and its new leader Marty Davis swam in during the mid-1980s – a sea of ever-circling sharks, looking for takeover targets. A world where too often you were only as good as your closing stock price, or your last quarterly earnings report. The winners in these battles were usually the winners in the battle for public perception. Simply put, the art of good PR had become more critical than ever.

At first blush, Jerry might seem like an odd candidate for success in this world. Although he was not an old man at age 53, he did in a way come off as a character from another time – the poker-playing product of Harrison Avenue in the Bronx, lacking a college degree, an ex-journalist from the era of manual typewriters at the cusp of the Computer Age. But what some might have perceived as potential weaknesses in the high-stakes world of Manhattan big business were actually Jerry's ace-in-the-hole: His trademark confidence, which only increased as he successfully navigated crisis after crisis, his street smarts, his strong relationships with the financial press in New York, where the top writers were his generational peers, and finally his battle-tested personal relationship with volcanic and mercurial Davis. After all, Davis – just like Jerry – had started his career as PR man, for Paramount back in the 1950s, and like Jerry he didn't have an elite university education. It was a world where the high-priced Ivy League recruits who cycled in – and frequently out – of the towering skyscraper on Columbus Circle were easily frightened and intimidated, but where Jerry Sherman thrived.

Marty Shea recalled that he and Jerry frequently laughed at the young over-educated executives at Gulf + Western – for example, when they tried to take advantage of one of the key perks of the job, taking in sporting events at the company's Madison Square Garden. "Madison Square Garden was just three subway stops from Columbus Circle," noted Shea, like Jerry a lifelong New Yorker. But on a game night, they'd typically see a fleet of corporate cars, lined up to ferry the executives right into the heart of Manhattan's notorious rush-hour traffic. "It would take these guys an hour-and-10-minutes to get there," said Shea, incredulous.

Shea said that Jerry's personality – that "ability to take a beating and smile all the way through it" – helped him to not only survive but flourish amid the volcanic personalities, but especially under Bluhdorn and then Davis, who had driven away so many of Jerry's predecessors throughout the 1970s. At the same time, the ability that Jerry had to relate to, and make friends with, everyone from CEOs to his restaurant waiter also made him a fixture at Gulf + Western as somebody whom everybody could trust in the firm's often tense environment.

Shea said that Jerry had a special knack for consoling co-workers who'd been dressed down or abused by Davis. He would tell his colleagues, "It's not your world, it's his world. We're here to serve him." At the same time, Jerry seemed to be just about the only person at Columbus Circle who could – on occasion, anyway – get Davis to back off his bullying of underlings or convince the boss that one of his ideas was unworkable. "Jerry would go to Davis and say, 'What are you doing that for?...You're intimidating people.'" Shea said that Jerry's most important role in the convoluted office politics of Gulf + Western was what he called "talking people off the ledge."

"He knew that you don't sweat the small stuff," said Carl Folta, who was a young PR executive who worked under Jerry during that era. But he said that Jerry would go to the mat with the fiery CEO if the issue were important enough. "He was smart and strategic about it."

Folta, who arrived in the Gulf + Western public-relations department and became a close friend of Jerry during a career in which Folta eventually became a chief spokesman for entertainment giant Viacom, said that Jerry was clearly already one of Davis' most trusted advisers by the time he arrived at Columbus Circle. He quickly learned that Davis gravitated toward executives with "street smarts" – a description that fit Jerry to a "T."

"It was clear that Jerry had knowledge of the media and the ability to deliver," Folta recalled. That meant quite a bit during the Davis era because not only was the G + W CEO a control freak but because publicity was the area where Davis had his early-career expertise. "He was in communications – he wasn't a lawyer or an accountant. So if you were in communications, he thought he could do his job better than you." The fact that Jerry was so skilled at the PR game, Folta recalled, gave him some room to maneuver with the boss that other underlings did not have.

Raising the Stakes

"Davis didn't want 'yes men,' but it was a Catch-22 because if you disagree too vehemently, you're gone." Jerry was one of the few who could walk on that high wire.

Jerry's ability to navigate the rocky shoals of working in the C-suite at Gulf + Western helped him to enjoy the benefits, particularly the company's influence and connections in the world of sports. The kid who'd changed the scoreboard numbers at Yankee Stadium in the 1940s was now a high-ranking emissary of the owner of two of his beloved New York franchises, the Knicks and the Rangers. The Knicks, despite the presence of players like the scrappy Phil "Action" Jackson, who would later become the NBA's winningest coach, were a mediocre team in Jerry's early years at Gulf + Western – but that changed dramatically in 1985 when the Knicks drafted the top player coming out of college, Georgetown's versatile center Patrick Ewing. Jerry's high perch with Gulf + Western allowed him to eventually become friends with Ewing and other players on the Knicks, a dream come true for the lifelong sports obsessive. Another iconic athlete of that era whom Jerry cultivated as a friend was the Giants' superstar linebacker Lawrence Taylor, who was the driving force behind Super Bowl victories in 1987 and 1991.

"One of the things that impressed me about Jerry more than anything else is that he would go to a Giants game in the afternoon and then he would come back and go to a Knicks game that night," Shea recalled. "I'd say aren't you tired of going to the stadium for games, and he'd say 'No!'" But Shea also observed that Jerry's passion for sports stopped in the cheering section. One of the perks at working for Gulf + Western at Columbus Circle was a sprawling fitness center that Bluhdorn had built on an upper floor, with not just treadmills but a squash court and a basketball hoop. Jerry wouldn't go near it, Shea recalled with a chuckle. "He didn't see a reason to exercise," he said. "At the end of the day, he is what he is. But he always had time for everybody. He was a very giving person."

For Jerry and Gulf + Western, owning the Knicks, the Rangers, and Madison Square Garden was also a fantastic opportunity to give back – and to boost the company's image through charity and good works. One event that Jerry was involved with, for example, was the 20th Annual Multiple Sclerosis Dinner of Champions, held in Madison Square Garden in 1992, which celebrated the likes of Muhammad Ali, Knick greats such as Willis Reed and Bill Bradley, and the teams' worthy opponents from Michael Jordan to hockey's Gordie Howe. Both through work and personally, Jerry supported numerous causes such as the survival of Israel, fighting for civil rights, and eradicating diseases. His name appears, for example, as a supporter on the Wall of Tolerance, a Southern Poverty Law Center project that joins him with others who've pledged to fight racism and bigotry.

Luckily, Jerry's love for the glitz of professional sports and show business was very much in sync with the vision that Davis had for the future of Gulf + Western. In January 1984, *Forbes* published a major profile looking at how the conglomerate had been transformed since the death of Bluhdorn, noting that the new CEO's massive divestiture of company assets was based on the new notion that "fit is more important than price." Thus, the article noted, Davis was in the process of putting forth a lucrative offer for the publishing firm Prentice-Hall, in order to match his vision that the new Gulf + Western would be centered around entertainment, publishing, and consumer goods while shedding the heavy industry that had been the original core in the 1950s and early 1960s. Already gone, for example, were the extensive sugar holdings that Bluhdorn had developed in his beloved Dominican Republican. ("We aren't in the sugar business because nobody here has a commodity mentality. Bluhdorn did, so he ran it," Davis said.)

In fact, some 46 companies worth a whopping $1.5 billion were sold off in those first 18 months, along with the $900 million investment portfolio that Bluhdorn had managed personally. "Everybody thinks of me as the great dismantler, but I'm not liquidating the company," Davis told the magazine. Like much of the coverage of the massive overhaul of Gulf + Western in those years, Jerry's name didn't appear – but the upbeat tone and the positive portrayal of Davis in *Forbes* (whose flamboyant publisher Malcolm Forbes was a longtime friend of Jerry) is a "tell," as they might say in poker, that Jerry was doing exactly the kind of job that made him so invaluable to his boss.

In 1986, some three years into Davis' run at the company, the groundwork that Jerry laid helped lead to positive profiles such as the nearly 3,000-word opus that appeared in the *New York Times* by financial writer Geraldine Fabrikant headlined, "The Orderly World of Martin Davis." The word "orderly" was clearly a reference to the contrast with the chaotic Bluhdorn, whose legacy loomed large, even in death. But Fabrikant's piece made it clear that Davis' focus on good public relations was what set him apart from his predecessor.

"Mr. Davis, perhaps because of his many years as a marketing executive, has cultivated a far better relationship with the media and with investors than did Mr. Bluhdorn." Fabrikant wrote. '"Mr. Bluhdorn didn't want to play the game,' said one financial executive. 'Marty understands the game. Now the company is simpler and there is more information about it available. That is extremely important.' Still, there are some nagging questions raised by Mr. Davis's management style. In 1984, *Fortune* magazine called him one of the toughest bosses in the country."

The article then features the obligatory discussion of Davis' hard-charging management style. Indeed, one of the problems that the Gulf + Western CEO encountered in assuming the reins was that the Paramount movie division, after so many stellar releases in the 1970s and early 1980s, harbored too much top, ambitious talent. Both Barry Diller, the studio head when Davis had assumed control, and a rising executive at Paramount named Michael Eisner clashed with their boss and eventually moved on. Eisner and Diller would be the two most powerful players in Hollywood by the 1990s – Eisner at Disney and Diller at Fox – and would factor again in Davis' future, but in the mid-1980s at Gulf + Western it had been a traffic jam of egos, and Davis has no intention of getting out of his lane. He would soon regret losing Eisner, who by the late 1990s was one of America's most celebrated business executives. "If I'm considered a tough manager, I think it is accurate," Davis told the *Times*. "I won't object. I am demanding. I want team players, I want results."

Raising the Stakes

The in-depth features about Davis and his makeover of Gulf + Western were at least partially the result of Jerry's close ties to the established business press and his ability to maintain channels with rising stars such as the *Times*' Fabrikant or Laura Landro, then a young journalist who covered the entertainment beat for the *Wall Street Journal*. Beyond that, the pre-internet world of business journalism was a complicated mix of publications – the big magazines such as *Forbes* and *Fortune* with their weekend deadlines, and a slew of trade publications – and Jerry had the experience and know-how to manage that. "You had to understand how these publications worked, and to craft a story line that resonated with the general public," Folta said. "Jerry understood that stuff." Landro recalled that Jerry was different from most of the other PR executives she dealt with, who often became angry when journalists bypassed them to try to reach top executives directly. "Jerry wasn't like that." Landro recalled. "He understood I had my own relationships with the executives at the company and its subsidiaries, and that if I needed to get a hold of someone, I would call them myself. But he was always ready to be helpful and chase them down if I needed it; and because he was so great in our dealings, it made me want to keep him in the loop and let him know what I was after - and what I was hearing. Often he could not comment, but he never let me put myself in a position where I was going to print anything stupid or wrong."

The story of the moment was that Davis had become a big believer in what was increasingly becoming a business buzzword as the 1980s wound down, and that was "synergy." The Gulf + Western CEO had no interest in judging potential assets on whether they were undervalued and could bring an immediate return, as his predecessor Bluhdorn had done. Instead, Davis, like many of his competitors at that time, believed that joining companies that fit together in logical ways – for example, a book publishing arm whose best-sellers could become box-office hits for the Hollywood movie unit, with cross-promotion on a TV network – was now seen as the winning long-term strategy.

Raising the Stakes

The fruits of that effort can be traced through copies of Gulf + Western's slick quarterly magazine, *One*, which Jerry played an integral role in producing for the company. A typical issue, from 1987, features a neon-bright cover with the line waiting to see a Paramount premier at Hollywood's iconic Grauman's Chinese Theatre (for a picture, Eddie Murphy's *The Golden Child*, which turned out to be something of a bust) and articles celebrating various entertainment offerings from Pocket Books or the newfangled MSG cable-TV enterprise. The publication put an exclamation point on G + W's message that its years as an auto parts firm were well behind it.

The goal for Davis was to become a media mogul. That meant pursuing high-priced potential mergers with other content providers; in the late '80s, Davis and Gulf + Western launched high-profile bids for Time, Inc., the iconic magazine company, as well as for RCA, which at that time was the owner of the NBC television network. Those failed, however, which ratcheted up the pressure on Davis, especially when Time instead merged with a rival studio, Warner

Brothers, to launch the Time-Warner media conglomerate in 1989, which was exactly the kind of synergy that Davis had hoped to achieve in his pursuit of the publisher.

In April 1989, Davis announced two major moves. First, the corporation would divest its commercial and consumer loan division, known as Associates First Capital Corporation; this, arguably, had been the most lucrative unit in Gulf + Western for much of the decade, pulling in as much as 45 percent of revenue, but it also had no place in Davis' long-term scheme. Instead, the corporate CEO planned to use the projected proceeds from the sale – at least $2.4 billion and possibly more – to finance more aggressive acquisitions in the media space. "We are down to a point now where we have to determine a direction," Davis told the *New York Times*. "Otherwise we're impairing the growth of both. We had to choose. I can't be married to two gorgeous women."

The other big move drove home the significance of the first: the Gulf + Western name was disappearing, to be replaced with Paramount Communications. It was the exclamation point on how much the high-stakes company had changed since Jerry signed on a decade earlier.

Indeed, Jerry's 10th anniversary was a reminder that – under two of the most volatile and demanding bosses in corporate America – he had survived in the pressure cooker longer than any of his predecessors, and probably far longer than he had expected. For a man who'd returned home from Barcelona just 15 years earlier with only a few dollars left in his bank account and had taken a job supervising a candy factory, the decade at Gulf + Western had brought financial security at a moment when his children were finally grown. As he approached 60, Jerry began to think seriously about an early retirement.

There's no doubt that the anxiety of working for the demanding Davis took a toll. On March 20, 1987, the *Wall Street Journal* published an article entitled "WHEN THE HEAT IS ON," purporting to be a look at the way that CEOs deal with the tensions that come with their jobs. One of the top bosses quoted in the article was G + W's Davis, who told the newspaper that his solution to the problem was (wait for it)..."patience." He spoke about how so much in life is stressful

– even waiting for a green light to cross the street – and concluded: "Part of the job of managing is managing stress...You learn to have patience and you can handle anything." The irony of his boss' comments must have killed Jerry. He framed the article and kept it for the rest of his life.

The reality was that at on least one occasion (and presumably more than that), Davis' bullying style had caused Jerry to offer his resignation. On August 17, 1987, after more than four years working under his fellow Bronx native, Jerry's frustrations boiled over in a letter than he sent to Davis – copying his then No. 2, Donald Oresman – on Gulf + Western letterhead:

Since, in recent months, your expressions of unhappiness and dissatisfaction with the way I manage the corporate communications functions at Gulf + Western have become more frequent, and the fact that our working relationship has deteriorated, I believe it would be in the best interests of both the Company and myself if I resigned as an officer and employee. I truly believe I have made major contributions to the success of the company, especially since your election as chairman and chief executive officer, and have

Demonstrated a special loyalty to the Company, to you, to Don Oresman, to Mike Hope and to the many others with whom I have worked closely these past eight-and-one-half years. Therefore, I hope we could work out a mutually satisfactory arrangement for my departure, including a timetable that would assure an orderly transition. Please let me know when it would be convenient for you to discuss this matter with me. (Signed) Jerry Sherman.

There's no hint in Jerry's files as to why his resignation didn't happen at that time. In the end, it may have just been a particularly bad day at the office. Instead, roughly two years later, Jerry signed an employment contract with Gulf + Western – with a fixed annual salary of $225,000 - that cemented his status at the company in the short term.

Marty Davis probably realized the same thing that Bobbi observed years later, that "he was lucky to have Jerry, that was my impression." Davis certainly didn't impress Bobbi back; she remembered him as "just a typical businessman, not very personable. He must have been smart at something but

I didn't see it. [But] Jerry respected his abilities."

Another major event that may have inspired Jerry to ponder both his legacy and his future was the 50th Anniversary Dinner of the New York Financial Writers' Association, which was held on June 15, 1988. In addition to some good-natured reminiscing about "The Follies Girls," the event at the Sheraton Centre Hotel was a chance for Jerry to be recognized with a Distinguished Service Award for nearly four decades of involvement with the group.

Indeed, the featured speaker that night, the publishing mogul Malcolm Forbes, was a friend from way back. Jerry had brought his family to the dinner, and they surged forward to exchange pleasantries afterward. Forbes leaned down to daughter Emily and asked, in an almost conspiratorial tone, "Was your father as great as everybody says he was?" Emily didn't miss a beat, shooting back: "If you don't leave your dirty socks on the floor!" The financial legend roared back in laughter.

Raising the Stakes

On Sept. 10, 1990, Jerry officially retired from Paramount, less than two months after his 60th birthday. His successor as vice president of corporate communications, Nicholas Ashooh, who'd been the chief PR executive at a New Hampshire utility, was just 35 years old, meaning that he'd been born around the time that Jerry was leaving the *Journal of Commerce* for his business career. Still, Jerry wasn't totally out of the game. The announcement mentioned that Jerry would again be launching his own firm, again called Jerry Sherman Associates. The listed address was actually his home on 12th Street. His very first client, the announcement noted, would be Paramount.

The timing of Jerry's departure might have been fortuitous for Jerry, young enough to enjoy his trips to casinos or to retreats like St. Martin in the Caribbean, where he and Bobbi would soon have a vacation home. But it was apparently awkward for Davis and for Paramount, which was the cusp of high drama as merger mania increased. The irony at Columbus Circle was that by slimming down the former Gulf + Western into a smaller media firm and highlighting its Hollywood connection, Davis had put his company at risk of being – for want of a better term – devoured. Some companies were still looking to become old-school conglomerates, like General Electric, the industrial-and-defense firm that beat out Davis in the war to own NBC. And so there was increasing speculation on Wall Street that Bluhdorn's old "Engulf and Devour" would soon be engulfed by rival suitors.

Indeed, such speculation had launched before Jerry had even retired. The bruising, high-stakes battle with Warner Brothers to purchase Time, Inc., which was a lead story on the business pages for seven weeks in the spring and summer of 1989 and only ended when a Delaware court blocked Paramount's bid of $200 a share, or roughly a 50 percent premium, kicked off rampant speculation that Davis' firm would now instead become a target. As *USA Today* put it in a headline on July 25, 1989: "Paramount now may be the hunted."

As the *USA Today* article noted, Paramount's huge pile of cash from selling off Associates First, which would have helped to pay for the proposed acquisition of

Time, Inc., now made it attractive to corporate raiders who could use the money to help finance a leveraged buyout. What's more, large foreign investors were eager to pay a premium to get a slice of Hollywood glamour, as Japan's Sony would eventually do later that very same year when it gobbled up Columbia Pictures. The story speculated that Davis might look for a friendlier deal the next time around, maybe in the newspaper industry (which had yet to launch into its long decline in 1989.)

"He tried to break up the Time-Warner merger and there was no Plan B after that," Carl Folta recalled. "And after that – because he was sitting on a bunch if cash – he became attractive to corporate raiders. And he didn't have a succession plan." Indeed, Davis' insistence in staying on in a major leadership capacity would prove a serious sticking point in several possible deals.

It didn't help matters for Paramount that, just at the moment that Davis had decided to go all-in on the entertainment business, the studio – which had been churning out hits throughout the 1970s and '80s – hit something of a slump. That was thanks to a string of flops such as *We're No Angels*, a spectacularly unfunny comedy starring the unlikely duo of Robert De Niro and Sean Penn. A lengthy article in the *Los Angeles Times* speculated that while Paramount had been a creative hothouse when Barry Diller and Michael Eisner had been running the studio, the emphasis under the Davis regime was not enough artistry and too much marketing and PR, the CEO's forte.

"Paramount has become more corporate, more faceless," one film executive told the Los Angeles Times, anonymously. "The residual personality cult from the Diller days is wearing thin. Those guys were storytellers who would call each other in the middle of the night with ideas. The new guys are just worried about making deals."

In the period after Jerry retired from Paramount, Davis had frantically looked for a major acquisition partner, and although his efforts inspired scores of newspaper clippings, he continued to come up dry. "I love Martin, you know that," a close friend told *Vanity Fair*. "But since October '89, he's had his thumb in his mouth. He bought some theme parks, some computer companies, some assets, but really? Nothing!" In the dangerous waters in which Davis and Paramount now swam, it was either eat – or get eaten. The half-hearted takeover bids from the likes of Carl Icahn and Boone Pickens that Davis had fended off in the early years would soon seem like child's play.

It was a stressful time, as the *Wall Street Journal's* Landro recalled: "They were not always happy with me over there - I can't tell you how many times I got screamed at by various executives over stories they didn't like. Jerry never did that. He'd occasionally let out a mournful sigh in our follow-up calls once a story came out, but that was as far as any ire went. It was his job to smooth over the ruffled feathers of executives and field calls from other reporters who had to follow a *WSJ* scoop."

The 1994 lengthy article about Paramount in *Vanity Fair* remains the most in-depth look at the boardroom drama in those years that Jerry was away from the company. It notes: "The Paramount drama featured not just Diller, (cable TV's John) Malone, and (Viacom's Sumner) Redstone but Ted Turner, David Geffen, Michael

Ovitz, Brandon Tartikoff, Laurence Tisch, Arthur Liman, and Felix Rohatyn, corporate chieftains such as Jack Welch of General Electric, all three major networks, European players such as Thorn EMI and Polygram, and Hollywood's Japanese pillars, Sony and Matsushita. There was even a cameo by the late Steve Ross (the former head of Time-Warner)."

The irony is that – as the story details – Davis in the years immediately after Jerry left Gulf + Western/Paramount was almost as un-strategic in his obsessive pursuit of deals and mergers as Bluhdorn has been – the only difference being that Davis concentrated his efforts solely on entertainment companies. After he was rebuffed by several major European publishing houses, Davis turned his sights on the record industry which had been booming for two decades and was about to plunge into an era of rapid decline, which no one saw coming. That didn't matter because, as *Vanity Fair* noted, while Davis "talked to almost all of them, including Polygram, Bertelsmann, and, before its acquisition by MCA, Geffen," no one had much use for Paramount. David Geffen's put-down was especially harsh. "He wanted to buy my company, and I basically said, 'Why do you want me? If you got rid of Michael [Eisner], Jeffrey [Katzenberg], and Barry [Diller], I'm just like them.'"

The recording industry wasn't the only thriving-but-soon-to-be-struggling sector of the media world that rebuffed Davis and Paramount; talks with the nation's newspaper chain, Gannett, also went nowhere. At some point during the early 1990s, Davis held talks with all three major television networks about a merger, again to no avail. At some point, the Paramount chief probably could have authored a book called *The Art of the No Deal*. But viewed another way, there must be 50 ways to ruin a merger, and somehow Davis got caught up in all of them – disagreements over who would run the merged companies, for example, or potential regulatory hurdles, or failure to agree on a price, or simply – as happened with David Geffen – a lack of personal chemistry, which seemed to happen a lot with the embattled Paramount CEO.

The biggest fish that got away from Davis was NBC, which seemed an ideal fit.

Raising the Stakes

Paramount had produced some of the Peacock Network's hit shows throughout the 1980s – most notably "Cheers" – and Davis had a scheme to take the resources of NBC News and create an international cable spinoff that would rival the then-cable-news leader CNN (which indeed would happen, not long after the *Vanity Fair* article, with the creation of MSNBC). Those secret talks between Davis and Jack Welch, the iconic CEO of NBC's then-owner General Electric, which dominated the era from the late summer of 1990 through 1992 when Jerry was away from the company, came to the brink of a deal but faltered over concern as to whether regulators would approve the transfer of the lucrative local TV stations that the network owned.

After the NBC talks fell through, Paramount's dealings became increasingly tangled and personal. Davis spent much of his time in talks with the Denver-based billionaire cable magnate John Malone or in shifting talks, occasionally involving Malone's friend, the TV legend and CNN founder Ted Turner, where it was unclear who was the pursuer and who was the pursued. At one point, according to *Vanity*

Raising the Stakes

Fair, a deal was at hand in which Malone's TCI would become an investor in Paramount and also Paramount would purchase some of TCI's properties, including its stake in the cable shopping channel QVC, run by the man who was increasingly becoming Davis' nemesis – his former studio chief Barry Diller.

After more than two years of merger mania that amounted to essentially nothing for Davis, Paramount was more the hunted than a hunter by the start of 1993, and the two key players eager to take over the entertainment conglomerate were Diller and an unexpected new player, Viacom, led by Sumner Redstone, who, mostly in obscurity, had turned a profitable movie-theater chain into a cable giant with popular channels such as the kids' network Nickelodeon and MTV. Redstone, nearing age 70, wasn't a household name yet – but those who knew him marveled at his tenacity, highlighted by an incident in 1979 when he survived a hotel fire by hanging from a ledge by his fingertips. As the takeover wars entered a new phase, Davis had two objectives: To block Diller, with whom he had a bitter falling out, and whom he saw as a stalking horse for the deep-pocketed Malone, and instead to negotiate a sale to Redstone's Viacom, hopefully for a minimum of $70 a share.

As the war reached its climax, there was one thing that was increasingly clear to Marty Davis: That the old school public-relations man needed better PR. Those who'd stayed at Paramount after Jerry retired said that his replacement Ashooh was simply too much of an outsider – lacking the right kind of connections in the insular, cliquish community of financial writers and corporate spin doctors – to shape the image of Davis and Paramount in this new era of celebrity CEOs where image influenced the stock price more than ever before. Folta recalled that Ashooh – recommended by Paramount's general counsel after some dealings in New Hampshire – and Davis were "like oil and water" when it came to working together.

On February 25, 1992, Paramount officially announced that Ashooh was leaving the company "to pursue other interests" and that Jerry – who had consulted for Davis and Paramount the entire time – would be returning as senior vice president handling corporate communications. Said Davis in the announcement: "Stanley Jaffe, the company's president and chief operating officer, and I are delighted to welcome Jerry back and look forward to his leadership in again directing the company's public relations. We are confident he will handle every assignment with the same skill, creativity and sensitivity that made him such a valuable member of our management team in the past."

Looking back, Jerry's co-worker Marty Shea wonders how much Jerry was actually retired during that year-and-a-half, anyway. "You would tell Marty that you're retiring and he'd say, 'fine,' and then the next morning he'd be calling you up to say, 'What do you think?'" With Jerry still on the payroll as a consultant, he recalled, Davis was seeking out his opinion all the time, so at some point during the merger crises it just made sense for him to return full-time. The journalist Landro recalled it was "sort of like that scene from "Godfather III" where Al Pacino says, 'Every time I try to get out, they pull me back in.'"

Raising the Stakes

Jerry's real assignment was to shore up the image of Davis in the eyes of investors, potential business partners and suitors of Paramount, Wall Street analysts, judges, and anybody else with a say in the company's financial future. The squabbles with the likes of Barry Diller or David Geffin – popular figures in the media at the time – had started to shape an image of Davis as a cold taskmaster, a bottom-line guy who squelched creativity, and a poor decision maker. But articles that appeared after Jerry returned to Paramount in early 1992 -- most notably the widely read *Vanity Fair* article, largely told from Davis' perspective – showed a softer side of the corporate leader. The story describes Davis as an antique car enthusiast, devoted to his second wife after "a nasty divorce," and even tells the story of his biggest tragedy, the death of his son, from heart failure, at age 32 on Christmas Day 1986. "I'm stunned that he mentioned that to you," a close friend told the magazine. "I thought he had just closed that out completely, because he has never referred to it."

The same unnamed friend also gives arguably the most humanizing quote uttered about Davis during his decade-plus at the helm of Gulf + Western/Paramount. "Martin can be the most charming man I know," the friend said. "Why he insists on creating this macho image, I'll never know. He has a very fragile view of himself. He's not a guy with a lot of innate self-confidence, and one of the ways he protects himself is keeping everybody away from him. It's very hard to get any real personal glimpse of him, because he's afraid to show it. There's a lot nicer person buried there he's afraid to let out. He's so afraid it'll give people the wrong image. It's as if he's [imprisoned] in the role." One has to wonder, more than 20 years later, whether Jerry – whose name doesn't appear in the *Vanity Fair* piece – was the unnamed friend of the CEO. Or, perhaps more likely, if Jerry played a role in connecting the writer Bryan Burrough with such a sympathetic source. Either way, this was the new public relations, and Jerry Sherman was proving that a veteran could be a master of the modern game.

Folta recalled that Jerry had returned to Paramount full-time in 1992 with an almost impossible mission, to make one of the more despised figures in the world of entertainment – "a guy who was generally disliked in the field" – into a sympathetic figure in the takeover wars.

Complicating matters was the fact that Davis' enemies in Hollywood – none more so than QVC's Diller – had such a good relationship with a fawning press corps that often told the story from their sides. Davis would sometimes fume at Jerry or the others in his publicity team over negative articles. "It's coming from the other side," Jerry would patiently try to explain to his raging boss, but typically Davis would have none of it. But Jerry absorbed the blows for his team. "He never let it roll downhill," Folta explained. "He protected his people."

For all his foibles and his failed merger bids, things started going right for Marty Davis and for Paramount at roughly the time that Jerry returned to the company for his second stint. In the end, Davis and his team engineered the outcome that they wanted, to make the most money for their investors and for themselves. But there would be an agonizing year of ups and downs to get there.

Raising the Stakes

At first, it didn't seem like it was going to be so complicated. By September 1993, Viacom's Redstone had raised his offer to acquire Paramount to $69.14 a share, which valued the entire company at some $8.2 billion. The price was just short of the $70 a share goal that Davis had steadfastly clung to, but it was still a substantial premium over the current price of the stock, which was in the mid-to-high $50-dollar range. "I didn't think it was worth quibbling over the last dollar," Davis told *Vanity Fair*. And Davis was slated to stay in the picture as CEO of the new Paramount Viacom International. The merger was front-page news when it was announced on a Sunday, Sept. 13, 1993. But it was hardly the end of the story.

Eight days later, Diller's QVC shocked the financial world by announcing a hostile takeover bid for Paramount aimed at upending the merger with Redstone's Viacom. Remarkably, the Diller outfit offered more than $80 a share – valuing Paramount at $9.5 billion – in the hopes that this was an offer that Paramount's board of directors couldn't refuse, regardless of the longstanding animosity between Diller and

Davis. Instead, Davis' side stalled, asking the QVC bidders to provide proof of the finances behind their offer (as Davis long suspected, Diller had some $1 billion in backing from John Malone through Malone's Liberty Cable, as well as $1 billion from another up-and-coming cable concern, Comcast). What's more, Paramount seemed more than willing to pull the trigger on a so-called "poison pill" provision in the company bylaws – a complicated procedure that had been invented during the 1980s to thwart hostile takeovers, which had very much been in vogue during that decade.

"We haven't seen good, old-fashioned street warfare like this" for years, Porter Bibb, a Ladenburg, Thalmann & Co. investment banker, told *USA Today* in October as the battle intensified. Davis' hope was clearly for Redstone and Viacom to increase their bid, although the Boston movie-house magnate seemed to lack Diller's zeal for the fight. Most experts thought the whole thing was headed for court, which placed an exclamation point on the importance of good public relations.

Despite Davis' keen interest in going with his ally Redstone and defeating his adversary in Diller, the battle was increasingly becoming a win-win for the Paramount team and the company's investors as the stock price kept climbing higher and higher. When Viacom upped its bid for the company to $10 billion in late October, QVC and its backers took the matter to Delaware Chancery Court, charging that Paramount was not treating its bid fairly, and seeking to get rid of the "poison pill" anti-takeover measures. Davis felt confident that he would prevail – so confident that he gave *Vanity Fair's* Burroughs full access as the decision was coming down on the day before Thanksgiving, 1993.

What happened that day was an unmitigated disaster. Davis revealed the Delaware Court's verdict to the magazine writer after getting a phone call. "They ruled in favor of QVC," he finally told Burrough, in practically a whisper. "No kidding. I'm not kidding." The writer stayed as Davis informed Redstone and then took the call from his studio chief Stanley Jaffe. "'Clearly we have lost the case" are Davis's first words. A burst of invective blasts from the phone. Davis holds the receiver away from his ear. 'Just relax,' he says. 'Hello?' He puts it down. 'He hung up.'" A few minutes later, Davis confessed: "There've been worse days, I know. I've just got to think of one."

It *was* a bad day, but it wasn't the end of the world. The judge's decision – which was affirmed in December by the Delaware Supreme Court – didn't automatically hand Paramount over to QVC, but it did set the stage for a climatic auction between Diller's firm and Redstone's Viacom. Somewhat predictably, the Paramount board recommended Viacom's latest, sweetened bid, which now stood at $10 billion, even though many Wall Street analysts were still betting on QVC to win. In early 1994, Viacom realized it needed additional firepower and engineered a merger with a then-highly successful young player in the entertainment space, the Blockbuster video rental chain, that would provide Redstone with more capital to complete the increasingly pricey deal, not to mention a stronger claim of the kind of entertainment "synergy" that financial experts were touting. That's more than a tad ironic: With the benefit of hindsight today we know – thanks to the shuttered Blockbuster or rival video-rental stores that exist on most U.S. shopping strips – that online streaming and other ways to watch movies at home would crush that industry. What's more, there was only dim awareness of the rise of the Internet, which was just a few short years away.

Here's how *USA Today* gushed about the developments: "Imagine, for starters, a movie about MTV's Beavis and Butthead, made at Paramount's studio, shown at theaters owned by the Redstone-controlled National Amusements, shown on Viacom's Showtime cable channel or its pay-per-view arm, and rented and sold at Blockbuster video stores. Paramount alone is a movie-making, TV-show producing, book publishing factory - a potential bonanza at a time when demand is expected to soar for all kinds of programming to dispatch onto the information highway."

Ironically, when the auction for Paramount came to a head in February 1994, QVC's bid was worth more – but Viacom's offer was larded with more cash and more protections for shareholders; thus, a majority of Paramount shareholders – primarily Wall Street traders and related institutional concerns – voted narrowly to accept Redstone's bid. Not only had Davis and his team, including Jerry, achieved their desired outcome, but at considerable profit. The takeover fight had caused the value of the stock held by Paramount insiders and executives to nearly double. In the longer view, an investor in Gulf + Western/Paramount would have seen his wealth increase 14-fold from the end of the Charlie Bluhdorn era through the Viacom merger.

However, during the merger machinations the plan for Davis to somehow preserve his role as a CEO in the new venture fell by the wayside. By April 1994, Davis' handpicked second-in-command Stanley Jaffe was forced out and then Davis, too, tendered his resignation. That month, the now former Paramount chief announced the formation of a firm called Wellspring Associates, whose mission, he announced in a statement, "will be to identify and invest in entities in need of extensive restructuring in order to enhance the value of their assets by divesting non-core businesses and expanding core operations." The media contact for Wellspring Associates, as listed on the press release, was Jerry Sherman. Jerry's roughly 15-year run at Columbus Circle was finally over and, despite occasional light work such as this, he was essentially retired. He had accomplished so much, it was hard to believe he was just 63.

Epilogue: King of the Hill

As successful as Jerry had been during his career in journalism and public relations, he was arguably even more successful in retirement. It didn't hurt matters that the 1990s were something of a golden age for Jerry's sports teams – including his now favorite team the Knicks. Jerry was often courtside as Manhattan's NBA team made a couple of runs into the NBA finals with Jerry's friend, their star center Patrick Ewing.

What was surprising about Jerry's retirement, though, was that the kid from the Bronx finally succeeded in finding happiness outside the city, in his majestic home overlooking the central Hudson Valley, nearly two hours north of New York. Although in fairness, the move north was arguably more likely to have been Bobbi's doing.

Raising the Stakes

As my father Bryan Bunch – who with his wife Mary had also moved up the Hudson Valley, on the other side of the river near Poughkeepsie – recalled the story, Bobbi was in the market for a spectacular vista, and so she called a real estate agent one day when she was feeling claustrophobic after so many years on West 12th Street to make an unusual request.

"I want to live on the highest mountain in New York State," Bobbi supposedly declared. The agent informed her that the tallest peak in the Catskills region would be Slide Mountain. "Then I want to live on top of Slide Mountain." The man on the other end of the line had to persuade Bobbi that Slide Mountain wasn't particularly habitable. But he had another property on the market that fit the bill: An expansive log cabin that looked down on Hudson River and that spectacular valley, not far from New Paltz. Because it had a very high ceilinged, enormous living room with bedrooms on the balcony, it was – for a log cabin – much like the Aaron Copland barn that the Shermans occupied on Shady Lane

Farm Road, the last time they had lived outside of a city.

Unlike the Shady Lane Farm years, Jerry adjusted – although it helped to keep the former homestead on West 12th Street as something of a *pied a terre* for basketball games or the occasional star-studded event in the city. Up the Hudson, he worked to make the log cabin his home. "One thing that Jerry did was he put the temperature in the swimming pool up to 97 degrees," Bryan Bunch recalled, maybe with a trace of exaggeration. "That pool was hot. I guess Jerry didn't like cold water."

He did still love to gamble, however. The 1990s also brought a big surge of casino expansion in the United States, and Jerry and Bobbi took full advantage – traveling frequently to the new Mohican Sun gaming palace that was opened by the Native American tribe in southern Connecticut. In the spirit of their trans-Atlantic adventures of the 1970s, the couple also took to the high seas and cruised around the world, crossing the ocean again on the Queen Elizabeth. Usually by the end of their journey, my dad recalled, they were always best friends with a cabin boy or someone from the crew.

One destination that Bobbi and Jerry fell in love with was the Caribbean Island of St. Martin, the perfect respite from the harsh winters of the central Hudson Valley. For a time they had a time share on the island getaway, then eventually purchased their own home where they entertained their friends from New York and made new ones.

In retirement, however, there would still be one last PR job for Jerry Sherman – fittingly as the 20th Century came to a close. On October 5, 1999, Jerry called his contacts at major newspapers and wire services to announce the death of Martin Davis, who was described in the *New York Times* obituary as "the fiery executive who reshaped the unwieldy conglomerate Gulf + Western Industries into the entertainment and publishing giant Paramount Communications." That fire had finally caught up to Davis at age 72, as he died of a heart attack. His family had asked Jerry to serve as the businessman's final spokesman. After all those warnings back in 1979 that he might only last at Gulf + Western for a matter of months, the trust between the two men had lasted literally a lifetime.

Perhaps it was because he'd had the good sense to retire early, Jerry survived longer than many of the men he'd worked with. In addition to its soothing river valley views, the log cabin overlooking the Hudson was geographically halfway between the homes of his grandchildren – who helped to keep him young. Later, Jerry and Bobbi moved even closer to Emily and her two boys, both of whom turned out to be baseball pitchers *extraordinaire* in their high-school years. Jerry's long love affair with sports was now kept very much alive as he and Bobbi intensely followed the baseball careers of Jasper and Arlo. David's boys, Isamu and Daniel, although farther away in Westchester, also were able to make frequent visits to the Sherman's homes near Albany.

The family patriarch's health didn't begin to seriously decline until the dawn of the 2010s, when Jerry celebrated his 80th birthday. He finally succumbed on November 24, 2013, at his home. Like most of his generation, his biggest legacy is arguably the flesh and blood he left behind, including his four grandchildren.

Not long after, many of Jerry's surviving friends gathered for a memorial luncheon to look back on the life and times of a colleague who had straddled two worlds, who used a recipe of Bronx street smarts and common sense and unflappability to become an almost Jedi-like master of corporate spin in a bewildering era of dizzying corporate mergers and CEOs with Paul Bunyan-sized egos. Without a college degree, Jerry had outsmarted many stuffed-shirt, obsequious, or downright scared younger executives with their Ivy League degrees. From the day he hung out his shingle as a public relations man in Midtown Manhattan in the 1950s until his retirement as a top executive four decades later, the business had changed – because people like Jerry Sherman led the way. Today's corporate pitchmen, tasked with making their bosses look good in a dizzying digital media world, are following the broad brushstrokes that pioneers like Jerry had set down for them years earlier.

It's easy for folks to be cynical about the world of corporate "spin," and Jerry could share those sentiments at times, even laugh about it. Again, I'm still reminded of Jerry's framed quote, one of the many things he left behind: "In the PR game, the days are tough, the nights are long, and the work is emotionally demanding. But it's all worth it, because the rewards are shallow, transparent and meaningless."

But the truth is that Jerry believed in what he was doing, and with good reason. He had mastered the art of making other people feel better about themselves, whether it was a captain of American industry looking to reshape his image or just a kid getting a football player's autograph on Christmas morning. The reality was much closer to another framed quote that Jerry held onto, written in fine calligraphy, under his name. It is from the Bible, 2 Samuel 18:27: "He is a good man and cometh with good tidings."